A LIFE IN WORDS

HENRY HOLT AND COMPANY   NEW YORK

STUDS
TERKEL

TONY PARKER

Henry Holt and Company, Inc.
Publishers since 1866
115 West 18th Street
New York, New York 10011

Henry Holt® is a registered
trademark of Henry Holt and Company, Inc.

Library of Congress Cataloging-in-Publication Data
Parker, Tony.
Studs Terkel: a life in words / Tony Parker.
p.   cm.
Includes bibliographical references.
1. Terkel, Studs, 1912– .   2. Broadcasters—United States—Biography.
3. Authors, American—20th century—Biography.   I. Title.
PN1990.72.T4P37   1996   96-2962
791.44'028'092—dc20   CIP
[B]

ISBN 0-8050-3483-8

Henry Holt books are available for special promotions and premiums.
For details contact: Director, Special Markets.

First Edition—1996

Designed by Kate Nichols

Printed in the United States of America
All first editions are printed on acid-free paper. ∞
10   9   8   7   6   5   4   3   2   1

Studs Terkel interviews courtesy of Mr. Terkel and WFMT-FM, Chicago.

Use of excerpts from the audio cassette anthology *Four Decades with
Studs Terkel* produced by Tom Voegeli and published by the HighBridge
Company, St. Paul, Minnesota, is gratefully acknowledged.

For him—and her—and him
and for Margery, always there.

Contents

STUDS TERKEL:
A Brief Chronology

1912   May 16; born in New York City. Third and youngest son of Samuel and Anna (Finkel) Terkel. Real name: Louis Terkel.

1932   Ph.B. from the University of Chicago.

1934   J.D. from the University of Chicago.

1939   July 2; marries Ida Goldberg. One son, Paul.

1945   Begins radio program *The Wax Museum* with WENR, Chicago. Runs through 1947.

1950   Begins television program *Studs' Place*. Runs through 1953.

Stage appearance in *Detective Story*.

1952   Begins radio program *Studs Terkel Almanac* with WFMT, Chicago. Runs through 1953.

1954   Begins radio program *Sound of the City* with WLS, Chicago. Runs through 1958.

Begins radio program *The Studs Terkel Show* with WFMT, Chicago. Program is still running.

1956   *Giants of Jazz* published.

1958   Stage appearance in *A View from the Bridge*.

1959   Stage appearance in *Light Up the Sky*.

1960   Stage appearance in *The Cave Dwellers.*

1967   *Division Street: America* published.

1970   *Hard Times: An Oral History of the Great Depression* published.

1974   *Working: People Talk About What They Do All Day and How They Feel About What They Do* published.

1977   *Talking to Myself: A Memoir of My Times* published.

1980   *American Dreams: Lost and Found* published.

1984   *"The Good War": An Oral History of World War Two* published. Wins Pulitzer Prize.

1986   *Chicago* published.

1989   *The Great Divide: Second Thoughts on the American Dream* published.

1992   *Race: How Blacks and Whites Think and Feel About the American Obsession* published.

1995   *Coming of Age: The Story of Our Century by Those Who've Lived It* published.

Introduction

I first met Studs Terkel ten years ago, when I was staying with my wife in a small town in Kansas, where I'd gone to tape-record interviews with its inhabitants. They were to form a book eventually published under the title of *A Place Called Bird*. Some months before I went, Julian Browne, then of the London *Sunday Times,* asked me if while I was in North America, I'd try to get an interview with Studs Terkel in Chicago, for a feature article about him they wanted to do. Yes I would, very much, I said, particularly as I'd admired his work for a long time—and he might agree to see me because he'd once given a kind review, some years before, to an earlier book of mine, *The People of Providence,* in the *Sunday Times.*

When I phoned him from Kansas, asking if I could fly up to Chicago to interview him, in those days I wasn't aware of his phenomenal memory. I was consequently somewhat taken aback when as soon as I said my name, he said "Oh yeah, you're the guy who wrote that book about the people who live in the housing blocks in London, right? Sure you can come and interview me—only on one condition though." "What's that?" I said. "That I interview you too" he said, "for my radio show."

Which is what happened. First I interviewed him—feebly and ill at ease, overwhelmed by his chiaroscuric and orotund personality. Then he took me to a recording studio, where he stunned me by producing a copy of *The People of Providence* in which almost every inch of text was confettied with his underlinings, and every blank space in its margins filled with notes of questions he wanted to ask me about it. I felt he knew the text better than I remembered it myself—and also almost instantaneously came under his spell as soon as the recording of the interview began, and found myself happily burbling away to him as though I'd known him all my life.

Afterwards, discovering my wife and I were staying overnight in Chicago before flying back to Kansas the next morning, he was insistent we should join him and his wife Ida for an evening meal at a bustling French restaurant. The food and the wine and the conversation were all exhilarating and we stayed until long past midnight: by which time, like so many others before us, we felt the Terkels had become among our closest friends.

I met him on several occasions subsequently when I was in America, working on other projects. Two years ago, I was in Chicago again, and asked him if anyone had ever written his biography. ''No'' he said, ''there've been a couple of people tried, but nothing came of it.'' ''Would there be anything in trying to do something along the same lines the way you do your own books?'' I said. ''You know, interviewing your friends, people you work with—and you yourself, trying to get details of your life, how you work, your ideas about how to interview people and so on?'' ''Heh!'' he said quietly, ''heh, that's not a bad idea. . . .'' ''Who do you think might be able to do it?'' I said. He jerked up his head, looked at me, and grinned. ''Oh you crafty bastard!'' he said. (Obviously he wasn't aware my astrological birth sign is Cancer the Crab; and one of the characteristics of Cancerians is they approach things sideways.)

Three months later, I returned once more to Chicago specifically to discuss the idea in more detail with him, when he had time to do it, having by then delivered the manuscript of his latest work *Coming of Age* to his publishers. As he'd promised, he'd prepared a list of names for me of thirteen people who he thought might be willing to be interviewed about him, including—he said typically—three who ''won't have anything good to say about me at all.'' (In two cases he was wrong, and the third was someone who was out of the country.)

Returning to England, I made appointments by letter and telephone to see in Chicago, New York and England not only the people whose names he'd given me, but others whose names *they* gave me—and in the following year I talked with a total of twenty-four people about him. I also talked alone with him in fifteen hour-long sessions—usually in his office. There he unfailingly wore his standard "uniform" of open-necked red-checked shirt, pullover and dark jacket, and entwined an elastic band round his fingers while he talked, eventually letting it slide down to join the other rubber bands which were already forming a bracelet round his wrist. But sometimes also our conversations were at his home: on occasions there he was in pajamas and dressing gown sitting in an armchair because he wasn't feeling well, but had refused to cancel our meeting on the grounds it would mean my having to rearrange my schedule of appointments for the day. And we talked together as well in restaurants and cafés, and walking along the streets. In all I tape-recorded twenty hours of conversation with him. Sometimes he was noisy, sometimes didactic, sometimes comic, sometimes somber, sometimes prolix, often repetitive, sometimes succinct—but always thoughtful, imaginative and reverberative.

It was difficult—no, it was impossible—to find anyone who had anything but the mildest of criticisms to make of him. Occasional—and they were very occasional and rare—critical remarks would be written by not-very-well-known reviewers of his books: but of his character, by far, the sternest judge of that was himself. Large portions of this book must, I know, read like an endless flow of hagiographic reminiscences of him by his friends. But despite my constant attempts to stem the flow with the most comprehensive assurances I could muster to reassure about complete concealment of identity if they could only tell me something, however trivial, to his detriment, I was unable to learn of anything at all that he'd ever said or done which had wounded or even discomforted *anyone.*

Even worse in this respect—or, of course, an even better indicator of his nature—is something which I experienced about him myself, regarding the twenty-four people I mentioned earlier whom I'd talked with about him, some of whose names he'd suggested. I never once told him either whom I was going to see, nor afterwards whom I'd seen. Nor did he ever ask me: but quite naturally from time to time one or other such name would come up in conversation. When it did, I wouldn't be secretive, I'd say "Oh yes, I've seen him (or her)." At which, Studs would merely nod his head and say "Oh good." He never once then said to me

"What did he (or she) say?", but instead continued our conversation on some other subject, quite naturally and without effort.

And one further, final, astonishing, thing. He neither asked when he agreed to my doing the work, nor asked when he knew I had finished the manuscript, to see it.

To him, then—to use some of his own words from his acknowledgments at the front of one of his own books—"a profound salute."

1

Working Colleagues at Radio Station WFMT

Norman Pellegrini, Program Director

Linda Lewis, Secretary/Personal Assistant

Jim Unrath, Producer

Stephen Jones, Recording Engineer

Lois Baum, Associate Program Director

Norman Pellegrini, Program Director

He wore a light blue shirt and a plain dark red tie. Tall, dark haired and quiet spoken, he sat at his desk relaxed and self-assured.

—WFMT is Chicago's Fine Arts Radio Station, and I've been program director here for more years than I care to remember—but I suppose since you ask I'd better confess and say it's forty-five. In my early days after I left college I briefly thought of trying to become an actor—but when I began to study for it, I realized it wasn't my *métier,* I was far too self-conscious for the stage. So I moved into radio instead, and it's something I've never regretted. Nor, obviously, have I regretted coming here either: it was more or less my first job, and it's been my only job. Not long after beginning I moved into programming, and not long after that I became program director, and that's where I've stayed. The station's changed ownership once or twice, but somehow I've survived.

We're part of the Chicago Educational Television Association, and in that way probably as little commercial as it's possible for anyone to be. We do carry some sponsorship and have some advertising, but we like to think that it's unobtrusive. For sure, in comparison with what you hear on other radio stations, or see on television, you could say it was near minimal.

Our daily programs are mostly classical music and talk, going out nonstop around the clock for twenty-four hours, with newscasts at mid-day and late afternoon and evenings. The scope and variety of what we air is pretty well endless, but we have a pattern of course—a season of operas, a season of plays, a season of concerts and so on. In the near future we'll be broadcasting Shostakovich's *Lady Macbeth* and George Bernard Shaw's *The Devil's Disciple* as well as a series featuring the majority of Heifetz's violin concertos. We also record, or take other people's recordings of performances at the Metropolitan Opera House, or by the San Francisco Symphony Orchestra for instance.

I won't bore you with an attempt at a full description of everything we do, but there's one other aspect of what we do which I'd like to mention, and that's our documentary and features programs. We recently did a four-parter called *Women in Music* which everyone concerned was very pleased with: it included women composers and their work, but it also covered what you might call the women in the shadows—those who were the wives or mistresses of, and influences on, composers and musicians.

So—that's WFMT for you—and the only thing I've not spoken of is of course what the station's most famous for, and almost synonymous with, and that's the name of Studs Terkel. In their time his broadcasts have been called *The Studs Terkel Show, The Studs Terkel Hour* and I'd guess a dozen other things too. But they no longer need any of that, so they appear in the published schedules with just the two words that matter— "Studs Terkel."

He was here when I came, and like everybody else before they meet him, I was awestruck at the thought of working with him. And—again like everyone else again, I'm sure—the feeling lasted only around twenty-four hours. I remember the first words he ever said to me, though I can't remember what occasioned them. They were "It's OK kid, it doesn't matter"—and he said them because I'd made some stupid mistake or other, and started to apologize. He just brushed it off. And he's always been like that ever since. Everybody'll tell you the same. "It's OK kid, it doesn't matter" . . . I think that sums up his personality, and says how he approaches life. *Of course* it matters—*to him,* about *his* work, because he's such a perfectionist. But at the heart of it is that he takes the responsibility himself, he doesn't try to shuffle it off on to someone else or make out they're to blame, not ever.

You'll often read in descriptions of him that he's known here as "a free spirit." The expression's used so frequently that if it's not in the first paragraph, you start to look down the page for it. Well I like to think I'm the first person who ever coined the phrase and brought it into use. Because that's certainly what he is. No one here tells him, or has ever told him, what to put in his program, because he doesn't operate that way. He ranges where his fancy takes him, and I find his output still as spellbinding now as I did when I first heard him. What his secret is I don't know, and I don't think anybody knows. In fact, I'd make a guess that if you asked him he'd say something like "Secret? What secret? What are you talking about?" Maybe that's his secret—that he doesn't know there is one.

I suppose what drives him on still, and so remarkably at his age, is his genuine curiosity about people, no matter who or what they are. And it's matched somehow with his almost total lack of interest in himself. He doesn't have a sense of self-importance that's in any way inflated at all—yet if anyone would be entitled to have it, surely it would be him because of his achievements. Such an ordinary looking little guy, and though I don't think he uses it consciously to get out of people what he's after, which is usually some expression of something they've never given thought to before, maybe that's part of the reason people feel at ease talking to him.

With Studs it's question, question, question—and then the next question and the next. What does this person think? Why does he think it? What made him the person who thinks it? His curiosity is endless, and it's honest curiosity into how people are, it's never motivated by jealousy or envy.

You know when he called his memoirs *Talking to Myself,* he hit on the exact and appropriate title for it, because that's what he does. You'll see this small white-haired figure in the distance coming along the corridor towards you, and you're often not sure whether he has someone with him, perhaps just behind him, or not. Because he's keeping up this stream of conversation all the time. And if there isn't anyone there, he's doing it with himself. He frames what he's thinking about with words, he tries them out for size and sound. As you pass he'll give you a greeting, and then as he passes on into the distance he's still talking. A musician'll tell you that for him, his head is always full of music: and it seems for Studs, his head is full of words—monologues, dialogues, group discussions, information-exchange, everything. I've never met anyone else remotely like him in the whole of my life.

Linda Lewis, Secretary/Personal Assistant

Small, brown haired and brown eyed, she was always smiling, welcoming and helpful. Laughing, she said shyly no one had ever interviewed her before and she was sure she wouldn't be able to think of the right things to say, but she'd do her best.

—Well, let's see. I was born and raised here in Chicago, in a suburb in the south of the city. I've been working here three and a half years now, and I did a whole lot of other things before this, working for different companies who did this and that, being usually a secretary in a general office. I worked for a Catholic publishing house where I did some typesetting, and also I worked in the subscription department of some of the magazines they published. Then I was doing secretarial work with a manufacturing company that made steel shelving, and I was with them eight years until they had to reduce staff and I was laid off. Before that I was at high school. When I was a girl my big ambition was to be a ballet dancer, but I'm one of nine children and there was no money to send me to dancing school. I married young and I was a housewife for a few years but then my marriage broke up and I didn't have any children, but I didn't want to sit around all day so that's when I started to work.

One day a friend told me there was a job going at WFMT Radio Station and I thought that sounded kind of interesting, so I applied for it. After a couple of interviews I got taken on, again in just a kind of a general secretarial capacity but not specifically here in the programming department. They gave me a guided tour of the place, and as we were going down the corridor where the studios are I happened to look into one of them through the big glass side windows that they have, and I saw an interview was taking place and the interviewer was Studs Terkel. I recognized him because I'd seen him on television and his picture being in the papers and so on, and I said "Oh my gosh! Does Studs Terkel work here?"

So naturally I thought this would be a pretty interesting place to work, because I might run into him one day. He was someone I'd always wanted to meet: I'd read several of his books, and become a fan of his for the first time when I read the one called *Hard Times* that my former husband had brought home and which I thought was pretty good and not like anything I'd read before.

When you come to work in a concern of this sort, as a general rule you move around from one department to another doing secretarial work as it's needed where it's needed. You might have a few months in advertising, then be moved into accounts or whatever, and that's how it goes. But I think I'm a fixture here now, not only in this job but as Studs' secretary and personal assistant. I'd certainly put up a resistance if they tried to move me from it, I can tell you that!

We have a close working relationship, and although the job can get pretty hectic at times as you can guess, I enjoy it so much that nothing else would be the same. He's unlike anyone else I've ever worked for in fifteen years, and I regard myself as his caretaker. I don't mean I nursemaid him because he doesn't need that, but all my cabinets and files you see around everywhere are to do with all the different aspects of his work, the people he knows and meets, and where they are and how he can contact them. For example I already have one on you.

He has an incredible memory himself, but every once in a while he wants to find some person or some thing in a hurry, and that's where I come in. He's impatient with detail, and what he has to feel—and what I think he does feel now—is that he can leave things to me because I'll have it all at my fingertips. At the beginning of each week I prepare a schedule for him of what he's going to do—his upcoming interviews and who they're with and on which days, and details of meetings he's going to attend and speak at, and who's coming here to meet and talk to him— and then give him reminders at the end of each day of what he'll be doing the next day. He gets through a tremendous amount of work. It'd be tremendous for someone of any age, but for someone of his age, well it is, it's just incredible. But it's never too much for it to be depersonalized. He'll always remember to ask you each day if you've got a cold, how it is: or if your sister's not been well he'll ask after her. His memory for that sort of thing's fantastic.

As you'd expect, he gets a tremendous amount of mail, from all over America and all over the world. Fan mail, requests for advice, invitations to involve himself in causes, speak at conventions, lecture at universities—oh the list's endless, and if it all got to his desk in two days he'd completely disappear from sight. So part of my job is to sieve it through:

I don't touch things marked "Personal" or "Private" or "Confidential," but for the rest I've had to develop as well as I could a sense of which things are very important for him to see and tell me what to do about, which are important and he should deal with them at a time when he's not under great pressure, which things he should at least see and decide if he wants me to follow them up for him or not, and which things can be ignored. I think by now I've got it right, because as far as I know there've never been any comebacks.

The same applies with the telephone. People'll call up and ask can they speak with him, and I have to be very polite and tactful in finding out who they are and what it is they want, and whether to put them through to him or take a message or what. When you think of how many people he knows and is friends with, I reckon that can be classed as quite an achievement.

What's so great though is that Studs is not a complainer—and more than that, he isn't temperamental. He has his off days of course, but then don't we all? He doesn't feel too good, or something's gone wrong somewhere, and when he comes in I can tell straight off that he's going to be a bit grumpy that day and won't want to be too bothered with things—so I make sure that he isn't. And as for him not being temperamental—well, I have one or two friends my own age who work with or for people not even as famous and well-known as Studs is, and they tell me what trouble they have in learning to handle the storms and squalls that go with being a celebrity of one kind or another.

So I'm very lucky that there's none of that with Studs, just none at all. He's in no way overbearing, not ever, to me or anyone else. He's human and humane, and I've never known him different. Some days if he doesn't have a lunch engagement and I tell him I'm going out to get a sandwich or something for my lunch, he asks me will I bring one back for him—and when I do, we sit there happily eating and chatting about home or family or what's in the papers or on TV. And he's just what he is, a very likeable and ordinary guy. I told him one day that I was reading *Race*, because naturally it was particularly of interest to me, being black as I am. And he starts asking me my opinion of different parts of it, of what certain different people had said. *Him* asking *me* what *I* think—and yet you know, there didn't seem anything special about it, he was just naturally interested.

. . .

Can I add something? I appreciate being interviewed. Like I said, I've never done it before, it's always me who fixes up the interviews for other people, so thank you.

Jim Unrath, Producer

He sat behind his large desk in his tidily arranged office in a swivel chair, his fingertips pressed together under his chin while he talked. A burly, amiable man with a deep voice.

—I've worked here with Studs for thirty-five years, and I've enjoyed all of it. I see him almost daily, and always have done, and if we've ever had a serious disagreement about anything, well I don't recall it. Studs isn't the kind of man you have bad-tempered arguments with: I don't, and so far as I'm aware nobody else here ever does either. I've never once heard him bad-mouthing anyone, I just don't think he has it in his nature. All of which makes for a good day-to-day atmosphere, and I know the rest of us will all tell you the same.

In the early days I took more of a technical part in things, and was often in the control room running that side of Studs' broadcasts with another engineer, but as equipment has improved it's no longer necessary for me to be there and Steve Jones runs it on his own. Technically of course Studs himself has never been very good—or perhaps a more accurate way of putting it would be to say that he's always been downright awful. It's ironic, really, that here's this man who's become rightly world famous as an interviewer with a tape recorder, when in fact his relationship with tape recorders can only be described in one word, which is adversarial.

Not only is he never sure when he goes out with one to interview somebody whether what he calls "the goddam thing" is working or not, but quite frequently is he so never-quite-sure that in fact it's not, and he comes back with a blank tape. Whenever possible we try to avoid letting him loose on his own outside, but that's not always possible, specially with his conversations that he has in the streets or backstage at theaters. We've tried everything we can—modifying, or with sophisticated engineering, to give him something that he can keep in his pocket and can make recordings with by having to press only one small button—but even then, sometimes he'll forget to press it or press another one instead. You wouldn't believe his ineptness with all things mechanical. Even when he's here in his office he'll suddenly start yelling for help, and Linda his assistant will rush into his office to see what's the matter— and what it is is he needs a new ribbon in his typewriter and can't put it in himself.

It still creases me up with laughing when I remember doing the prize-winning radio documentary "Born to Live"* with him. When we'd outlined the script and worked out all the tapes we were going to cut together, we found the best time to work was between one o'clock and six o'clock in the morning, because between those hours we were the only people here and we had the use of all the studio equipment entirely for ourselves. There was one particular tricky part which involved the use of three different turntables—music to one, distant background singing on another, and voice commentary from the third. I couldn't manage the transfer of all three at the same time onto the master tape myself, so I asked Studs if he'd take charge of one and, when I gave him the signal of a head nod, if he'd play the few bars of the music by pressing a button to let the sound come in. We get to the moment the first time and I nod at him—and he says "Now?" I said "Look Studs, don't say anything because it gets recorded on the master. Just press the button." "OK OK" he says, "I understand." We do it again, we get to the point, I nod—and he says "I don't say anything, I just press the button?" "Studs" I say, "please don't speak when I nod—just *press the button*." "OK OK" he says, "now I've got what you mean, OK let's go ahead." Once more we run back and start again, come to the point—and I nod. And he nods back at me in total silence. But he doesn't press the button. I'm not exaggerating—we did it more than thirty times before—at last at last—he did it right. But you don't get angry with him. It's all so human, and you know he'd never explode at you, so in time that quality he has rubs off and when you're with him you become like that too.

One of the fascinations for me in working with him is how he's always

* "Born to Live" won the 1962 Prix Italia radio documentary prize.

thinking of new ways of presenting things. "How do you think it would be if we did this in this way, do you think that would make it more interesting for listeners if at that point we put in a little music?" It might be jazz, it might be classical music, but it'll always be something that gives a kind of unexpected lift or tone to the program. He's particularly good I think when he's interviewing someone who's written a book that he's found interesting, because he goes about preparing for it most meticulously. He underlines paragraphs or sentences or even single words, and makes columns of notes on the blank pages at the front of a book, so that when he comes to talk to the author he's almost as familiar with it as they are. And they take that, rightly, as a compliment, that he's paid so much attention to what they've written and given so much thought to the questions he's going to ask them.

His questions are never destructive or argumentative, they're explorative. "Could you tell us a bit more about that?" And if it's a story or an autobiography "And what happened then?" It's always like that, Studs sounding genuinely interested. Because he is: if he isn't, he doesn't interview them. I've heard him many times say to a writer, "We could talk for hours about this"—and that's literally true, there are at least twenty questions Studs has ready in his annotations, literally for almost every page of the book.

There's his fabulous memory too of course. For things, for people, for conversations, sometimes I think that nothing ever passes him by, and he can recall it years later. Why or how it should be like it is, is a mystery, and it's a capacity like no one else's I've ever come across. He doesn't do too many documentaries these days, but when he does it's an extraordinary experience to work with him on one. He'll say something like "You remember that guy in Alabama I talked to, what was his name? Albert Jackson or something like that, and he told me that story his grandfather used to tell him about the red dust from the quarries covering the leaves on the trees? Well maybe we could use that here." And you realize with a shock that he's recollecting something that's on a tape he recorded ten years before—and sure enough, if you hunt it down in the library, eventually you'll find it and that's just what the man said.

Or he'll surprise you with the width and depth of his knowledge too. He's like a walking encyclopedia. Someone not long ago he was interviewing said something about the Dutch abstract painter Mondrian, and Studs is immediately in there with a question like "Yeah, and isn't he the guy whose work's sometimes used for color-testing of someone's eye-sight?'' You think to yourself how can one person encompass so much knowledge about so many different things, remembering too that most of them must be self-taught?

He's a showman with a big ego of course, but that's part of what's endearing about him. Linda's the one who's most exposed to it, but she handles him wonderfully. He's not a show-off showman, and we all tease him about it and he enjoys it. And his ego's not in any way an overbearing one. I'd say words like "flamboyant" and "full of life" were better terms for capturing how he is, because there's nothing of the "great I am" in him, not one bit of him at all.

He's enjoyable to be with and to work with, and I think that above all his outstanding quality is he makes you feel that he enjoys working with you too.

Stephen Jones, Studio Recording Engineer

One side of the control room was a glass panel, through which he could clearly see everything that was happening in the studio. The rest of it was a huge array of turntables, mixing and dubbing machines, and banks of tone and volume levers and switches. Everything was arranged to be within quick access from his central desk, where he sat in command, sipping coffee from a polystyrene beaker as we talked.

—Talk about Studs for half an hour? Sure, whenever you like. Right now, OK, suits me—give me a moment to finish this rewinding, then go straight ahead. Ask me anything you like.

I've been here ten years, and I engineer all Studs' programs for him. He calls me "the demon engineer," and I'm pleased about that, because he hates all things technical and doesn't understand them. And doesn't want to and doesn't try to, which is great because he never interferes, which there's nothing worse than. I've had a little experience of that sort of thing in the past and so have some of my friends who're at other stations in the same line of business, and we all feel the same way about it. We're engaged to do a job and we know how to do it, and when someone who knows less about it than you do comes poking his nose in and saying you ought to do it a different way, that's about the most infuriating and stress-making situation you can be in. So, like I say, Studs is a great pleasure to work with because there's nothing of that sort of thing ever with him.

He's a perfectionist in his interviewing, he likes his work to be the best possible that he can make it. I'm a perfectionist in sound recording, and I like it to come over in the purest sound I can produce it. So there you have it and that's why we suit each other.

My very first impression of him when I came was one of amazement. I couldn't understand why a man more than twice my age should be working—and not just working, but working so hard. I thought "Why isn't he retired?" But in the years since I've completely changed my attitude, and now my thought is always that I hope when I'm his age, if I live to be that, I hope I'm working too. It's a complete attitude change, I have to say that, and it's come from working with him. I can't explain it any better way than to say—well, not that it's inspirational, but that it's the way of looking at things he has, you know, that life's fun, that life's fun and work's fun and they're both of them somehow bound up with each other. And working with him, well it's somehow always more like a partnership in producing something. We hardly ever get across each other I suppose is what I'm trying to say.

There are occasional drawbacks and difficulties naturally, there always will be with any working relationship. The main one is the one I've mentioned, of our two different approaches and him not being at all technically minded. Sometimes he'll get to be a little impatient about it, say like when he's going to interview someone in the studio and he's exchanging a few ideas with them about how they'll start—maybe with a short piece of music, or the person reading a passage from the book they've written. He'll spend maybe a couple of minutes sorting it out with them and then he'll say "OK great, that's it, we're on our way, let's go"—and he can't understand that I then say I must have a little more time myself to run the tape leaders and mark the start and stop points. He doesn't mean any kind of personal criticism of me, and I understand that: but I think it baffles him that however good your technology is, you do need a few preliminaries to set it up.

This is part of his enthusiasm and his spontaneity of course, and why he's so good at what he does. He generates feeling in the person he has in the studio with him, whether they've never broadcast before or a hundred times before, that this is going to be great. It communicates itself to me too at the control panel—which I guess takes me back to what I was saying earlier about how when it's happening it hardly seems like work. It's something you want to do, from a technical standpoint you want it to be as good as it can possibly be.

Like pretty near everyone else who ever comes in contact with him, I'm always being surprised by the incredible store of knowledge that he keeps in his head. I don't mean for people only, but for things, for subjects which so far as you know he's not heard about or spoken about or read about or anything—and yet there he is in the studio talking to someone about their own special subject in a way that shows, without any kind of exhibitionism, that he has enough knowledge to hold a reasonable conversation about it for an hour or more.

To give you an example of what I mean, let me think a minute. Yeah, I know. About a couple of years back there was a guy came to Chicago, I've forgotten his name but he was a pianist from the Argentine and he was on a tour where he was performing something called "the New Tango." He was a very professional and accomplished player, and he had as his accompanist a young guy who if I remember aright was on accordion. He spoke only a few words of English, so there was an interpreter came along too, together with a couple of folk from the embassy and one or two others from the organizers of the tour. We were using the big studio, but with all those plus a grand piano and chairs for everyone to sit on, there wasn't much space. What there was was taken up with various mikes—one for the piano, one for the pianist, one for Studs to sit at near him, another for the accordion player, and chairs for everyone else.

Arranging where they should all go and how far away they should be from the different people taking part was some task, I can tell you. While I was fixing it all, I noticed Studs quietly talking with this pianist guy and once in a while, but not often, getting the interpreter to clarify a word or a phrase. The amazing thing was that this Argentinian, who'd looked pretty horrified at the whole setup which must have seemed to him like Times Square at rush hour, in five minutes he'd forgotten everybody else there and was chatting and smiling with Studs, playing little notes and chords on his piano to demonstrate things. They were in a complete world of their own.

And there it all was, almost an hour of talk with extensive musical illustrations on the piano, on the New Tango. And Studs' questions were informed and stimulating like they always are—"When did that first happen?" "How would that sound if you played it the old way, give us a demonstration." "Who was the first exponent of that?" And you think "Where in hell has he got all this stuff from? Old-time dance music, yes, he probably remembers that from his youth. But the New Tango? I'd never even heard of it till this guy came in the studio." He's unbelievable.

I'll make you a confession. I try and not boast about it, but now and again I do. You know what? Among my friends I'm a kind of a celebrity, because I'm not just a recording engineer: I'm *the* recording engineer for Studs Terkel.

Lois Baum, Associate Program Director

In her fifties, dark haired and fresh complexioned, she wore a plain white blouse and an elegant dark blue skirt as she sat at her desk and swung herself gently from side to side in her chair.

—Before I came here thirty years ago I was working in radio in Los Angeles. I'd heard of WFMT of course—it had the reputation then which it still has now, of being the best fine-arts broadcasting station in the country. I applied for and got a post as a junior editor and then after a while Norm took me on as his assistant and things have gone on from there. I don't have any one specific responsibility, any more than he does. We both involve ourselves in everything, depending on the ebb and flow of staff resources, and there are very few things which I haven't done at some time or another—with the exception of acting, I've never done any of that, nor ever wanted to. The part I like least I suppose is office work, administrative work—and the thing I most enjoy is the putting together of programs—documentaries, dramas, discussions and things of that kind, especially when they have some sort of sociological content.

What I mean by that is that if they have some relationship to society as it is today, portray some aspect of our late-twentieth-century world, then I'm most at ease with them. Coming as I do from a privileged part of society, I suppose I'm what some people might call an armchair liberal. But I don't like the inequalities and injustices in this great democratic society which we claim ours to be, and it dismays me that so many people choose to ignore them or pretend they don't exist. In a city such as Chicago you can pretend all's right with the world—if you have money. But if you don't have money, you know it isn't.

I had a strange upbringing, or strange in a way, in that my father, who was probably the most influential person in my life when I was young, was a man of conflicting ideas, all of which he held equally strongly. He and my mother came here from Germany in 1929 with absolutely no money, and in fact someone had paid for his passage for him—someone who already lived here, I think that was the system he came under—and he, my father, had first of all to work as a laborer to pay off the debt. He was a man with very little formal education—only up to about fourth grade or something like that—but he was a hard worker, and after he'd paid back what he owed he learned how to be a baker and by 1935 he'd worked hard and saved enough to buy his own bakery. He worked very hard at that too and made a great success of it.

When it began to thrive he and my mother had three children, of which I was the eldest. Like a lot of people who hadn't themselves been educated, he determined his children should be, and so we all were, going on to high school and college. I'm sorry, I've rather digressed here from what I was going to say about his character being complex haven't I? But for example he employed a large number of people in his bakery as it grew—people of all types and nationalities, Irish, Italian, West Indian, French, German, Chinese, everything. In my teens I often worked in my vacations too in this polyglot world if we were temporarily short staffed, and from my father I learned not to have any racial prejudice of any kind. But the one big prejudice he did have was against trade unions, and he wouldn't employ anyone if he found out they belonged to one. And yet, a further contradiction was this—he paid all his workers above trade-union minimum rates.

Then he sold the bakery and went into retailing, where again he did very well, and when he retired our living standard was a very comfortable one. This is what I meant earlier by saying I came from a privileged background, because I never wanted for anything at all. But somehow my own particular attitudes developed separately and differently, and I became what I am and who I am not from any conscious rebelliousness but instead from going along a line of becoming more aware of the political climate, I guess.

Being here, working here, and particularly working with Studs, has reinforced my attitudes, I'd say. I admire him for what he's done to bring to the attention of people, not only in America, but all over the world, the thoughts and opinions and dreams of ordinary people, of simple people who no one has thought of great importance before. His books are used as teaching tools in schools and colleges all over the country, and there's no way of estimating how many people's lives he's touched, simply by reminding us constantly that we're all related, we're all human beings living on the same planet, and that we must learn to listen to one another and respect one another if we're to survive.

When I first came, it was before he was known as a writer. I don't recollect exactly the date of publication of his first book, not off the top of my head, but whenever it was, he was of course already widely known as a radio interviewer and a writer of documentaries, as well as for his shows on television. I've always wished that he'd return to doing more radio documentaries, but I can see that in a sense his books might be considered as the logical successors to that aspect of his work. There are still many issues and problems in any big city anywhere, that would lend themselves to single-program treatment on radio, and he of course would be the ideal person to do them.

Working with him—and I have worked very closely with him for many years—has always been personally satisfying and rewarding, because he always makes you feel that you're sharing the experience together. Whatever the subject, out of that incredible storehouse mind of his he can bring so much to bear on a subject, look at it from so many different angles and in so many different lights, that your interest in it and commitment to it becomes as intense as his own. He draws on music and literature and philosophy and poetry and psychology and history—in any one of the fields of the humanities. In a society like ours which is increasingly concerned with notions like man-management and business administration studies and such things, I think core values are gradually being lost sight of.

Necessarily I'm generalizing about it, perhaps because I know his work so well. But he's a constant reminder to me in what I'm doing, of the importance in any documentary program of not setting an agenda and then going out to find material to fit it. If you do that, if you have preconceived notions of your own, then sure enough you'll be able to find the evidence to confirm them. But if you do as he's always done, let your material shape your program or your book or whatever, then I think you'll produce something of much greater value.

He surprises you the listener, or you the reader, with what he discovers in people, and where he discovers it—and he does that, I'm sure, because he constantly surprises and excites himself. And he makes the world a livelier place, and a more alive place, by doing it.

2

Higgledy-Piggledy: Studs Talking (1)

—No of course not, no sure, you're right. A lot of folk make that mistake. *Talking to Myself,* they call it my autobiography. But it isn't. I don't describe it that way myself. I describe it in the subtitle, I call it *A Memoir of My Times.* That's what it is. That's all it is. One thing leads to another in it, in subject matter. Anecdotal rather than chronological.

There *are* things in it that *are* autobiographical, sure, but they're incidental. They come in along the way you might say. There's more in it of me, me personally I mean, than there is in any other of my books though. Except in *Chicago,* I nearly forgot that. There's some autobiographical stuff here and there in *Chicago.* Only that comes in in the same way too: it's not chronological either, it's anecdotal.

Why've I never done a straight autobiography and why've I never let anyone else do one? I'll tell you. Two reasons, both genuine, both true. Certain things in everybody's life are in what might be called "the private domain." Things they don't want to talk about, things that cause them discomfort or embarrassment to talk about. One of the reasons might be they feel if they *do* talk about them, it'll not only embarrass them, it'll also embarrass and discomfit other people. As an interviewer you can sense this sometimes when you're interviewing someone. You get the feeling you're approaching some subject they don't want to talk about. So what do you do? You back off, right? You didn't ask if you could interview them for the purpose of causing them pain. You asked not because you're an inquisitor, but because you need to empathize with them if you want to find out what they're like. You don't want to expose them to prurient curiosity. I don't like people to invade my personal space, I guess I'd put it that way. I try not to do it to other people, so I expect other people not to do it with me.

Yeah, I did say there were two reasons. Well the second one'll sound maybe strange to some people—it's I don't find the subject of my own life of very great interest. I've met hundreds, no I've met thousands of interesting people, and I've been so caught up with them and fascinated by them and intrigued with them it's almost like there's no room inside me to be all that interested in my own feelings and thoughts.

I was thinking of this the other evening after we'd talked. You know, all the way along, all through my life, things have happened to me in no kind of order. Inconsequentially, you might say. My life has been higgledy-piggledy, you know what I mean? Without any formal shape or pattern, one thing following another with no particular plan to it. Good times, bad times. But mostly good. And you know something else? As soon as I've used that phrase, life being higgledy-piggledy, while I'm saying the words instantly one part of my mind's detached and is saying inside my head "That's a curious phrase. 'Higgledy-piggledy.' I wonder what its origin is, I wonder who invented it?" Heh, so what does that show me up as? A man who uses words without thinking? Or the opposite maybe, a man so fascinated by the sound of words he can't use any without being overconscious of them?

It's good though. I love words, I prize words, I always have. Reading them, using them, hearing them, listening to the million different ways people use them. They're endlessly fascinating. And you know something? I can pinpoint the exact moment they came that way into my life, and we'll come to it later, I'll tell you about it.

Well, you told me to look back through my mind like it was a photo album didn't you, yeah. I thought that was a good image. Childhood memories, memories of childhood, they *are* like that, it *is* like looking through an old photo album. You see people, groups of faces frozen a fraction of a second in time. You think to yourself "That's me, my parents, my brothers, but when *was* that, *where* was that? Who took it, why'd they take it, what does it mean?" That's the first picture I see: this group somewhere, this anonymous-looking group: my father with some of his teeth missing, my mother looking kind of prim and proper, and my two brothers, Meyer and Ben. Both of them older than me. And I'm standing in the middle, aged around fifteen I guess. And you know what? We're all happy and smiling like one big happy family.

Which we were not. We never *were* a happy family. And why? Because there were always problems with my mother. She was volatile, highly emotional, impulsive and that's putting it mildly. In law the temptation she had to say something hard or hurtful would be called "irresistible." Some of the abuse she gave to people was terrible, and no one ever knew who she was going to turn on next or for what. Then she'd be contrite about it and say she couldn't help it. Which was true, she couldn't. There was a wildness about her that made the home atmosphere always so tense. And the toll it took on my father and my brothers having to live with this person, not knowing from one moment to the next when she was going to explode, and about what, all our lives were heavy with it. I guess that's why the photo of a happy-looking family group has stayed in my mind. It's an irony you could say, an ironic symbol of what family life looked like, and what it was in reality not.

Another big moment for me was my first pair of long pants. I had them the day I graduated from elementary school. I was twelve, thirteen. That was the day life began. Before it I have an almost complete mental blackout. I think it's because as a boy I wouldn't let myself think of the unhappiness and stress at home. I tried to wipe that off the blackboard of memory: and I think I did that, I think I succeeded pretty well. So the result is what I have is not so much coherent memories as what might be called fleeting glimpses of urban boyhood.

I was born in New York. I remember playing in a street in the Bronx that wasn't so much a street as a community, a neighborhood: people of every race and nationality living side by side. I don't want to sentimental-ize it and say "in complete harmony": there was great diversity of culture and custom, but somehow people lived with it and with each other and had respect and tolerance more than I think they do now. Jews and Italians were the predominant groups, and there were Russians, Hispan-ics and many others. Oh yeah and particularly the Irish people too of course, I mustn't forget them. What does the inscription say at the base of the Statue of Liberty?

> Give me your tired, your poor,
> Your huddled masses, yearning to breathe free . . .

something like that. Well those were the people I grew up among, first- or second-generation immigrants, and their children. I remember them as people, just people, delightful, friendly, colorful. They had their problems, sure, but I was too young to know about things like that. Too young to imagine people even had them.

And I remember I felt ours was the only unhappy home—the only one among hundreds of happy ones. In the way kids do, I remember feeling guilty about it, as though in some ways it was my fault. I was the youngest you see, so I was the golden child, the favored one. So to me somehow I was always deep down the cause of the tensions and emotional beatings my father and brothers took from my mother. I'm not usually this introspective, at least I don't admit to being introspective. When I am though, I dwell on that subject, I think about it, I try to puzzle out why it should have been. Here I am, eighty-three, and I *still* think about it. These thoughts creep up on me. Isn't that strange? It makes me uncomfortable still you know, even after all these years. Now why in hell should I feel that? I've this notion—no, it's more than that, it's a fact—that I was the golden boy in the family. Not because I was clever because I wasn't, I definitely wasn't. But because I was sickly. I had asthma and I believe at one stage rheumatic fever, and then I went into the hospital for a double-mastoid operation which left me with perforated eardrums and these hearing problems I now have. That was the way they treated that condition those days, surgery. They didn't have all the wonder drugs they do now. Mastoiditis, you hardly ever hear of it, right? Huh, that's another bit of irony for you.

So anyhow like I was saying, I was the golden boy, everybody was kind to me, took care of me, looked after me, protected me. Even my mother, she didn't give me anything like such a hard time that she gave the others. Sometimes I think she even *liked* me. That was it, that was what made me feel guilty.

History is easier, facts are easier aren't they? My father and mother came from a town on the Russian-Polish border, Biatystok it was called: it was an industrial center for textiles and steel, and a transport center. It had a population of around a hundred thousand, and they were decimated by the Nazis in World War Two. Like many other Jews, they came to America in 1903 on the first big migration from eastern Europe: they were married but till that time they'd no children. My two brothers and me, we were all born here. I heard from someone, it must have been my mother I think, that one of them married on what they call the rebound from someone else. Maybe it was just one of her accusations she was always throwing around. He was a tailor, by all accounts a good one; he worked in a factory. He always made all the family's clothes. She was a seamstress, pretty nimble with her fingers, quick and neat and very precise. She worked in a garment factory too, but also she did a lot of private work. They were poor.

My father had bad health. I remember him always as an invalid: trouble with his heart, trouble with his lungs, having to be hospitalized, being in a sanatorium. He felt bad about it, about not being a good provider for his family, the way fathers should. He was good and kind and gentle and I liked him very much. When he died, which was when I was a teenager, that was the greatest grief I've ever had in my life. He'd been ill a long time, and I guess all of us knew it was going to happen. However much you try to prepare yourself for something though, when it happens there's no way you can stop the pain of it. My brothers were as fond of him as I was, and he of them. He was a warm loving character, he always seemed to give and receive affection wherever he went. Yeah. Gee.

Only you know, unkind it might sound, but I'll be honest about this, and I'll say I wouldn't know how my mother felt about it. There was . . . you know, I think there was something *wrong* with her. She couldn't help being like she was, I don't know, maybe it was something in her genes. She was a strange, strange woman. All through my father's long periods of illness and not being able to work, there must have been many times when she was the only person bringing an income into the home. She worked very very hard to see we had sufficient to eat, had proper clothing and schooling and all that. But what nobody got from her was warmth and love, or at least not a display of it. She had such a readiness to hurt people, emotionally I mean: I've never been able to understand it.

She lived until she was eighty-seven. During the last few years of her life she was in an old-people's home. When she first went there one of the social workers said to my wife Ida, who'd also in her time been a professional social worker, "My, what a sweet old lady your mother-in-law is!" And then, it can't have been more than about a month afterwards, the next time Ida visited, that same social worker called her into her office for a talk and she said "I don't know how your husband survived his upbringing. His mother's a monster!" I mean I guess that's fairly strong language wouldn't you say? But you know, I'll tell you something else. My brothers were both older than me and they've both died: like my father, comparatively young. But I've gone on like my mother, now I'm in my eighties too. So maybe it's her genes I carry, not his—and maybe one day someone'll say to you "Heh, what a monster that guy is!" That's a disturbing thought I have some days here in my head.

Like all kids I'd try sometimes to imagine my parents making love. Which they must have done, obviously, because they had children right? But like all kids, I never could. My soft kind gentle father loving and making love to that frightening woman? I laugh about it when we talk about it, but the idea didn't seem too funny to me, not when I was a child.

Let's see now . . . I remember another occasion, one of those snap-shot photographs we were speaking of. There was some kind of party or family gathering—someone's birthday perhaps—at the house of my uncle who lived here in Chicago. Everyone was talking, playing pinochle, socializing, about thirty people altogether I guess. Then suddenly—she was late getting there for some reason or another, I don't know what—suddenly between the open doors at the entrance of the room my mother appeared. And everybody instantly fell silent. There was a kind of a *frisson:* everybody's back stiffened like this. It wasn't anything she did, she hadn't even started to speak. Only just for that moment, for all those thirty people or so, time stood still. Everything stood in abeyance till it was known what she was going to say. And then all she did was smile. It was like she knew what effect she could have on people, even on people like them who were her family and friends. Then she just said something pleasant and ordinary, something like "Hi everybody, sorry to be late." You could feel the tension dissolve, the unspoken collective sigh of relief that went all around the room. She wasn't going to pick out anyone to fight with or humiliate, so everything would be OK. And the conversation picked up again. You know what it was like? It was like in the old days when what we called a phonograph and you call a gramophone, when someone put their finger on the playing arm to bring it to a stop—and then lifted their finger and it spun up into life again, you know how I mean?

How old I'd be then? Maybe eight or nine I guess. It was not long after we'd come to live in Chicago from New York. We did that because of this uncle, or uncle-by-marriage I should say to be strictly correct.

He'd married my father's sister. He wasn't a millionaire but he was a well-off guy and he wanted to help us. And so help us he did—he owned some hotels here in the city, and he leased one of them to my parents to run it for him. They weren't palatial places, but they were somewhere above rooming houses in general standard though. They provided my mother and father with a small but steady income to live on, and that was good of him to do that for them.

I've written about them, I've told anecdotes and stories around them in a couple of my books, some of the escapades connected with them with my brothers Meyer and particularly Ben. One was called the Elite: everybody pronounced it "the EeLight," and the other was known as the Wells Grand because it stood at the junction of Wells Street and Grand Street. They each had about fifty rooms, and chiefly it was my mother who ran them because my father was ill so much of the time. I've always said, and it's true, that it was growing up in those surroundings, more than any formal schooling, which gave me my education. That and my two brothers, no one could've been luckier than I was in that respect, that's for sure.

The eldest, Meyer, he was the studious one. He gave me the dope on English and Latin, he took me to the theater, introduced me to plays and books and reading. Shakespeare, Mozart, whoever, my first contact with them would have been through Meyer. He was seven years older than me. And my brother Ben, who was five years older, well he taught me the joy of life. He was a fun-loving, happy-go-lucky type of guy. He used to take me with him when he went dancing at the Dreamland Ballroom: through him I heard what has ever since been one of the great loves in my life, which is jazz. I first heard it with him when I was around ten. And he took me to the movies and the burlesque house and generally broadened my outlook. The two of them, all through when I was a boy, they laid the foundations for me of eclecticism, you know what I mean?

Both those hotels have long since disappeared. They've been pulled down and other buildings put up in their place. One of them was near Cook County Hospital that Sydney Lewis has just recently done her book on. In the days my mother and father had it, it was near enough the hospital, and cheap enough, for many young interns and technicians and student nurses to stay in while they did their training. They came from all over the United States. These days they'd many of them be from Africa, India, China and so on: it'd be a great place if it still existed to do a parallel book on to Sydney's. Have you met her yet? Oh, when you do you'll like her: she's a great young woman, she's good, she's going places.

There was one third big influence on me, and that was my English teacher at high school. He ran a marvelous course, and some of the things that guy taught us about I've remembered all my life. Scott's *Ivanhoe* was one, Coleridge's *Rime of the Ancient Mariner* another, Robert Louis Stevenson's *Treasure Island* and finally *Beowulf*. Anybody who can give a not-so-bright schoolkid a lifetime's love for a quartet like that must be some teacher, right? Oh and yeah there's another one I almost forgot, it's that poem about Sir Patrick Spens. You've not heard of it? Let's see how much of it I can recall after seventy years.

> "The King he stayed in Dunfermline Town
> Drinking his blood red wine
> 'Oh where can I find a good sailor' he said
> 'To sail a ship of mine?'
> Then up and spoke an elder man
> Who sat at the King's right knee
> 'Sir Patrick Spens' he said
> 'Is the best sailor who sails upon the sea.'
> And the King a letter wrote and signed it with his hand,
> And sent it to Sir Patrick Spens who was walking on the sand."

I love that part, "who was walking on the sand." Amazing how things stick in your mind.

> "Sir Patrick read aloud, and loud laughed he:
> But as he read a fear arose and blinded his ee—"

I'm not sure if I've got that part right, it's been such a long time.

> "Who is this, oh who is this
> Has done this deed so ill to me
> To send me out this time of year
> To sail upon the sea?"

And then he drowned. "And then lang lang may the ladies wait, With their gold cams in their hair." I think it's "cams," I think it's Scottish dialect, a word for "pins" or "combs" perhaps. Weren't there things called Border Ballads? Perhaps it's one of those, my memory's shaky on it.

The Ancient Mariner, that was always a favorite too: the melodrama of it, I guess. But often when I couldn't go to sleep—still now, sometimes when I can't—I let it run through my head,

> "Oh sleep! It is a gentle thing,
> Beloved from pole to pole!
> To Mary Queen the praise be given!
> She sent the gentle sleep from Heaven,
> That slid into my soul."

And then of course the most famous part, that's stayed with me always too.

> "The fair breeze blew, the white foam flew,
> The furrow followed free;
> We were the first that ever burst
> Into that silent sea.
> Down dropped the breeze, the sails dropped down,
> Twas sad as sad could be;
> And we did speak only to break
> The silence of the sea.
> All in a hot and copper sky
> The bloody sun, at noon,
> Right up above the mast did stand,
> No bigger than the Moon.
> Day after day, day after day,
> We stuck, nor breath nor motion;
> As idle as a painted ship
> Upon a painted ocean. . . ."

And then here it comes, heh!

> "Water, water, every where,
> And all the boards did shrink;
> Water, water, every where,
> Nor any drop to drink."

Isn't that fantastic? it's like a surrealistic painting, the way he uses those words. And when was he, Coleridge? The first half of the nineteenth century. Incredible, fantastic.

You know what though, to go back a little, I've given you haven't I, earlier on, a very dark picture of my mother? But I'm trying to be truthful about her with you. It's painful but that's how I found her, how I remember her. I'd like somehow to have come to know her better when I was older, you know what I mean? To have been able to sit down and talk with her sometime and tried to understand her. I guess that's something a lot of kids never had a chance to, did they? And they don't realize they've missed the chance until it's too late.

I think she came to America you know with my father like so many other people did: they were thinking they were going to start a new life, they were thinking they were going to make it big. The great American Dream. So many people had that. And it just didn't fall out that way. There was what there was for nearly everyone, the struggle for existence—my father's ill health, my brothers and me to bring up, dependency on her brother-in-law who *had* done well and was kind and generous enough to bring us all to Chicago and lease us the hotels to manage for him. It was humiliating to be indebted: it always is. I know it was a matter of pride for her that she finally paid him back every cent she owed. And it was through her own determination and hard work she did it.

She collected the fees for the rents of the rooms, she kept the books, she did everything. But it wasn't the life she'd hoped for and dreamed of when she first came. You have to understand this about people don't you? For most of them life's been a disappointment: it's only the lucky ones who've found fortune and fulfillment in what they're doing. I had a lot of grief, she had a lot of grief: and I don't think we either of us came to understand each other's lives at all. I should think some more about that some day shouldn't I? At the time though I was a kid, a boy clerk in a rooming house in a bustling city where the trolleys went all day and night up and down the street outside with their bells clanging. It was exciting, it was vibrant, it was life.

Let me tell you something else my English teacher did for me before I forget. When I graduated, he gave me two books. I guess he did the same thing for each person in the class. One was Olive Schreiner's *The Story of an African Farm* which I read and thought, and still think, is one of the finest modern novels there's ever been: and the other was a copy of *Roget's Thesaurus*. That one's always been one of the most significant and important books to me there ever was. You know I was telling you I could pinpoint the moment when words came to be central in my life? Well this was it, this was my epiphany.

Did you know the guy who did it was an Englishman? His parents were Huguenots but he was born in Soho somewhere around the end of the eighteenth century. Isn't that something? One of the greatest books ever given to the English-speaking world, a treasure chest of stimulation and delight, and it was done by a physician of all people, when he was seventy-three! You used to have a radio program didn't you in Britain, asking people what gramophone records they'd take with them if they were marooned on a desert island, *Desert Island Discs* was it called or something of that sort? And you could choose one book as well? Well if they ever asked me I'd not have to think hard about it, because for sure it'd be *Roget*. You know, whichever page you let that book fall open at, right there in front of you there'll be a dozen words at least that'll set your imagination up and running. Isn't that something?

Yeah and I've just thought of another teacher who was good. I remember with affection a young woman we had as our debating teacher. She used to divide the class into two halves, and then give us a proposition, this half to speak in favor of it and this half against. We'd choose the team, and then she'd tell us the subject. I remember I was put up as the lead speaker one day for our side, and she said "OK Louis, you're to oppose the motion which is this." And then she wrote it on the blackboard. It said: "Resolved: That capital punishment should be abolished." I stood up and I said "Miss, I am not going to speak against that motion. *For* it I will speak, yes, with all my heart. But *against* it no, no way." "Louis Terkel" she said, "now you listen to me. This is a debating-skills class, it is not a class on whether we wear our hearts on our sleeves or not. If you want to learn debating skills you will, with the help of your classmates, work out what points you are going to make and how you are going to make them. And then you will do just that. Otherwise you will not attend this class. Is that understood?''

She faced me down on it. And so I made my speech opposing the motion, and the seconder made his, and we took a vote on it at the end. And for God's sake, would you believe, our side carried the day and the motion was defeated. Which we'll call another of life's ironies, shall we?

There was another one I remember, a subject she introduced. ''Resolved: We should grant the Philippines their independence.'' I don't think I was on one of the speaking teams on that one. I remember sitting there in class and thinking to myself ''Heh, who are we to talk so patronizingly like this, about 'giving' independence to people in their own country which we'd taken off them after they'd lived there thousands of years?'' In these times, you know, that young woman teacher'd have been considered a dangerous radical, a subversive, trying to undermine what we like to think of as democracy. Not in those days, though to one of her pupils at least—and I'll not have been the only one. She was someone who thought education meant opening a few windows, encouraging you to think for yourself, listen to other peoples' ideas and respect them. Do people like that still exist in our education system? I'm sure they do. Or I guess I'm sure they do.

What did I have in mind when I graduated from high school? I hadn't any clear idea. One part of me wanted to go in for the law—I'd read about the great Clarence Darrow, the defender of the guilty and the oppressed, the man who defended Leopold and Loeb and saved them from the electric chair. I saw myself as some kind of heroic figure like that, so I enrolled at the University of Chicago Law School. You know what? I hated it. Instead of finding myself involved with the study of criminal law it was torts and malfeasances and real-estate transfer and all that stuff. I took this part of this examination and passed it, and then I took the next part and failed it, and had to take it again to pass it—and that's how it went, on and on. Those were unhappy, uncomfortable years: I seemed to be getting no place with my life, and not enjoying it either. Like I told you, I was no scholar.

This would be early to mid thirties, towards the end of, and after, the years of the Great Depression. I remember in one of my books, *Hard Times*, I asked a man who'd been around the age of fourteen in those years what he remembered of them, and he came out with an answer which I thought was pretty good. He said he'd always taken "Depression" in its medical, clinical, psychological sense: they were years when everyone was downhearted and pessimistic. That's what he thought, he'd never construed it in an economic sense. That hadn't occurred to me before, but it was true, there *was* that meaning to it as well.

So there I was, passing out of law school with my law degree and not wanting to practice, being uncertain of the future, and being depressed about it and about myself. And my greatest ambition in life then was the same as everyone else's—security, to have a good sound solid nine-to-five job. Can you imagine that? That was what I most wanted to do. Something ordinary, something that'd give me security, pay me a good-enough wage to live on. I wanted to be able to go to the ball game every once in a while or a movie when I felt like it, and read books and be like every other guy. That was the height of my ambition when I was twenty-two, twenty-three years of age.

What represented the kind of job I most had in mind was something in what I think in England would be called the civil service. One time I came close to attaining one too. It was a clerical job known as a fingerprint classifier working for one of the FBI's departments in Washington under J. Edgar Hoover. I put in for that. When they got my application they made enquiries about my background, and I only discovered these details forty years later when I saw my file under the Freedom of Information Act which came into force in 1975. One of my professors in law school had told the FBI agent making enquiries about me that when I was his student he didn't consider me to have been "the best type of boy." When that was reported, that sank me: my application was rejected. I've often reflected if that hadn't happened, who knows? I might have spent my life working for J. Edgar Hoover and the FBI. Another thought I enjoy the irony of.

Instead I got a different less sensitive job with the government. I became a lowly paid clerk in the department counting the issue of what were called "Baby Bonds." Then later I got to be a supervisor on one of FDR's government-sponsored unemployment surveys. It was of Omaha in Nebraska. It didn't go so far as actually *going* to Omaha—nothing with so much imagination in it as that—but supervising a team of young women and girls—it was always men who were supervisors and women and girls who did the donkeywork—of trawling through column after column of figures to find out which were significant and which weren't.

This was all a part of the New Deal and Roosevelt's efforts to rebuild the economy of the country after the Depression. I was a tiny cog somewhere along the line in that vast machine, I guess.

But life took a significant and unexpected turn for me then. Course I didn't know it, I wasn't aware of it. One of the other supervisor guys I met and got friendly with, we found we had a great interest in common, which was theater. He was much more into it than I was: he was involved with a workers' theater group who were doing a play, a left-wing play by a writer called Clifford Odets. It was called *Waiting for Lefty,* you've heard of it? They'd just started their rehearsals and he asked me would I like to go along. He was the producer of it, and I said sure yes why not, so he took me. And the next thing I know I'm in the play! Someone was sick and didn't appear at rehearsal, and I'm the only guy around so they hand me the script and tell me to say the lines and then learn them—and that's it! I'd never even thought of acting before. So there you are, that did, it altered my whole life. We did a few performances and I had one of the minor parts: but it was around the time soap operas were starting to get popular on the radio. And in the audience one night there was a guy who ran one of those serials, and he came around backstage afterwards and asked me to look him up.

So I got a job in this long-running radio show. From there I got other parts offered me—usually gangsters because of the low husky menacing sort of a voice I had. Then someone took a chance on me, and one of the stations offered me my own radio show.

It was during that period, when so many different things were going on, that one which was of course the most important of all occurred. I met and married Ida. By profession she was a social worker, but in her spare time like I was she was interested in film and theater. It was on one such occasion that we met. In those days social workers, they were rightly looked on as aristocrats: they were very special people. I always regarded her in the first days of our acquaintance with a certain amount of awe. You should ask her if she'll talk to you. I don't know whether she will or not, not for publication. But go ahead, ask her. She can only say "No," right? It's her choice.

We've been talking an hour? No, really—an hour? OK we'll stop there shall we? Before we do though I'll tell you something. My saddest moment was when my father died. I was riding the streetcar a few days later, sitting on my own. Not thinking about him—then suddenly I did,

and I burst into tears. Can you imagine that? I was helpless, uncontrolla-
ble, I had to get off the streetcar. I've never had a moment like that in
my life, not before or since.

Some sadness of course, yes, but not of that sort. Of occasional dis-
tances between me and those I hold most dear. Sadnesses, regrets, we all
have those don't we? Sure. I'm tired I think. You too? Yeah.

3

American Friends (I)

Mike Royko, Newspaper Columnist

Florence Scala, Community Activist

Beverley Podewell, Actress

M. N. Newman, Newspaper Reporter

Nancy Newman, Public Relations Consultant

Peggy Terry, Poverty Action Group Worker

Mike Royko, Newspaper Columnist

—"*Well I'm sorry sir*" *his assistant said when I called up the offices of the* Chicago Tribune, "*I don't think it's possible for Mr. Royko to arrange an appointment to see you for you to talk about Mr. Terkel. It's all seat-of-the-pants stuff the way we work here. Oh sure—I'll ask him for you, call me again tomorrow around 8:00 A.M., OK?*"

That second time, the message was different.

—*Mr. Royko says can you make Thursday afternoon around four sir?*

A deep-voiced tanned-faced man with graying hair, he sat in a black leather recliner behind a mound of papers and books on his desk, word processors within reach at each side.

—No problem, I've always time for talking about Studs, take as long as it takes. Janice'll field all my calls, go ahead.

How long and how? Oh, it must be thirty-one, thirty-two years now I guess. I hadn't long been writing my column, when I had this call from him: he said how much he liked whatever it was I'd written that day. That was something for a young journalist setting out on his own in the news-paper world, I can tell you—a phone call from the well-known radio show presenter Studs Terkel at WFMT. He asked me in for an interview, we did it, then he took me for lunch, and he was a real friendly guy. We'd a whole lot of ideas in common, and we discovered too we lived not far away from each other near the lake. So from then on one thing led to another, he and his wife came to our place for dinner, another time we went to their place, and that's how it's gone on ever since.

I was a fan of his radio shows already then, and that's something's never changed. He must be one of the most skilled broadcasters I've ever heard, the way he mixes music and talk together. That's in his documentaries. Then there's the way he interviews people, that's something else again. I never met anyone with so many fields of interest and so much knowledge about them. That's what he gets from his preparation beforehand. It's amazing: he can be talking about interpretation of music with some great orchestral conductor—and then next time, he's just as much at home talking to a guy who's a long-distance train driver. He always knows what are the right questions to ask. And he lets them speak, he's interested in what they've got to say: and that's no act, he *is* interested. There's another thing you notice in his radio interviews too: they seem to be getting rambling and discursive, and you think "Oh he's forgotten the point he was asking about." But he hasn't. He has a road map in his head, and he goes off on some sidetrack, but he knows exactly where the highway is and comes back to it.

Another great gift he has is putting anyone—everyone—so at ease they feel they can talk. I could never imagine someone replying "No comment" to Studs when he asks them a question. As a journalist I'm a facts-and-figures man myself, I've got to have that kind of information background to a piece even if I'm not going to quote it. But he doesn't work that way: he might not know what year someone was born, maybe not what decade even—but he knows where their heart is, he knows where their soul is, and where to find the things in them they care about.

That's about him as a technician, that's about his abilities as a professional, that I admire very much. But there's another side of him that I've come to know too, over the years we've known each other. They're the qualities he has as a human being, as a man, as a friend. Not so many people know about those, because maybe they haven't directly experienced them. Nelson Algren did, he was always supporting him and trying to bolster up his self-confidence when Nelson had a bout of depression, which was pretty often. What most people don't know is that he frequently helped him out financially as well.

I was a recipient of what it meant to be Studs' friend too. Fifteen years ago I was forty-seven, my wife was forty-three, and suddenly she died. I'd never in my life had anything like that happen to me before, and I felt like I'd never get over it. I didn't want to do my column, I lost all interest in work, I completely lost interest in life. If it hadn't been for only a handful of people, I don't know where I'd have finished up—in the gutter, most likely, I think. And of those people who helped me pull through, Studs was the principal one. He didn't give me any of the cheer-you-up kind of help he did with Nelson, it was more subtle and indirect than that. He'd call me up and ask me to meet him for a beer after work, and when we met I'd generally say something about my column that'd appeared that day and how dissatisfied I was with it. And he—he'd read it of course—he didn't give it overpraise, which we both knew it didn't deserve, but he'd say something like "I liked the point you made about such-and-such" or "I thought it was effective the way you compared so-and-so with so-and-so." He pulled out the few positive parts—or sometimes the parts that hadn't worked so good—and talked them over with me. What that did was it began to get me interested in my work again, and thinking about it and caring about it. That was clever of him.

Then after a while he did something else too. He suggested to a publisher I should write a book about Mayor Daley, and all the things that people didn't know about that were going on at city hall. Well, I was a journalist-writer, an articles and features man, a columnist: I'd never written a book in my life. The concept of it, the whole idea of it was beyond me, I was scared by the idea. But Studs twisted my arm and he kept on twisting my arm until finally I agreed, I said OK I'd give it my best shot. And all the way through he made me keep on talking to him about it, putting me up when I was down about it, giving me advice when I asked him for it. So the book finally got done, and it was a success—a big success. And that was down to him—that I started in on it, that I didn't give up on it, and that I saw it through to the end.

In my opinion, the man's a giant. He's well known, sure, more or less all over the world, and especially here in Chicago of course. You only need walk down the street with him and someone'll recognize him and call out a greeting. But that still doesn't mean they realize the true value of him here, because they don't. He's got his radio program and that's one whole career in itself—and then on top of that he's got the books he's done, and that's another whole gigantic career too.

I don't think Chicago people truly recognize what they've got in him, and I'm not saying that because he's a friend. I'm saying it because it's true, and I guess it's because people make their heroes out of figures in other fields than literary ones. Look at Michael Jordan the basketball player—a legend in his time. OK, a good basketball player—and people pay a hundred dollars a ticket and up, just to watch him play basketball. He opens a restaurant—"Michael Jordan's Restaurant"—and those nights except when he's playing for the Bulls people go and eat there because they're hoping he might be there and they might catch a sight of him.

And Oprah Winfrey—now she's not even a Chicagoan, but she moved here to help her career along, and it did. I like her, she's very talented, very nimble, she comes over on TV as a likeable person—and what happens? Her own personal cook, for God's sake, she does a book and calls it *Oprah's Favorite Recipes*—and it sells more copies than all of Studs' books put together! What sort of a society is this we're living in, I ask you, you wouldn't think it credible now would you? But so there you are, there you go. No one if they were a stranger would get within a half mile of Michael Jordan or Oprah Winfrey—*or* Oprah Winfrey's cook. But anyone who likes can come up to Studs and say "Hi Studs, how're you doin'?" and they'll get a friendly reply.

There's one thing I'd like to add on about him as well, to what I was telling you earlier about how he supported his friends, me when I needed it, Nelson Algren when he needed it, and a good few others I'm sure nobody hears about, leastways not from him. I didn't know him at the time of McCarthyism when he was blackballed and couldn't get work, but I know people who did. They all say the same thing though—*he* didn't ask nobody's help or sympathy for what he was going through, which must have been pretty rough, I can tell you, pretty rough indeed. He made a joke of it, played the clown, like he always does about things even now. He was no dangerous radical, no way—but since they labeled him one, then he made a joke out of telling people he'd been un-masked, and that that's what he really was.

Next time you see him, tell him something for me, will you? Tell him Mike Royko says hello.

Florence Scala, Community Activist

*The wide suburban street leading out of town from the center of the city was
lined on each side with a row of shops and dingy apartment blocks. At a corner
a mile and a half along it at a junction with a lesser road, her neat little house
stood on its own, a small preserved memento of the area years before. It had been
a restaurant, and her front door opened directly into it. There were wall murals,
a bar with fittings and furnishings, and a long table and chairs.*

*Gray haired, straight backed and clear voiced, she sat at it with her hands
clasped in her lap.*

—Gee, I've known him a hundred years, all my life it feels like, all my
life. Everyone who knows him will tell you the same too I'm sure, because
that's the way he makes you feel. But no, seriously, let me think: I'm
seventy-six and I first saw him when I was sixteen, so that's what, sixty
years?

At that time, along with some friends I was a voluntary worker at a
place called Hull House, which was a settlement that had been founded
in this area by Jane Addams around the turn of the century. Most of the
people who lived in these parts were poor black families, and we worked
with them on literacy classes, educational projects, basic housecraft, arts
programs, amateur theater productions and things like that. Studs wasn't
famous like he is now, not in those days, but he was involved in some of
the stage things and if I remember it right, that's how we came across
each other.

Then the war started, I married my husband who went in the military
to Burma, and didn't come back until 1946. I kept on with my voluntary
work at Hull House, but I didn't see much of Studs at that time because
he was in the army also, and also he was busy building up his career in
radio. When my husband came home he worked for the city on new
housing projects, mostly for black people who were coming up here from
the South to find work, and I went on working at Hull House. At that
time we had a good relationship with the city—we had a community
planning board, on which we all worked together on plans for the rede-
velopment of this whole area here. It was held up as a good example of
cooperation between administrators and local people, and could have
been called a model of its kind, because that's what it was.

And then, at the beginning of the 1960s, the city dropped a bombshell on us. Without even telling us, not so much as mentioning it to the community planning board, they made a public announcement one day, on the radio and in the press, that they were going to demolish this whole area, and rehouse the people who lived here in all different parts of the city. And for why? Because they'd chosen this as the place where the new University of Illinois and its campus was to be: and also they were going to build an expressway through to take traffic out from the city.

By then Studs was a well-known figure, and we asked him would he give us some help in publicizing our campaign to try and stop this thing happening. Being who he is and the kind of man he is, he didn't say "Yes, sure" just like that: he said he'd come down into the district and interview people who were residents of it, and ask them what *they* felt. He didn't put them into a frightening situation by asking them to the studio, he went there among them. They all, nearly one hundred percent, said they didn't want their community split up, they liked their neighborhood: and he broadcast a lot of that, as well as having different people from Hull House to do more formal interviews.

We lost the battle of course—what chance have ordinary people got? I remember he always used to say to me "Florence" he used to say, "Florence, we must stand together against the behemoth!" But he gave us so much help, and one thing that came out of it was that we were able to get over our point of view. The city hall people always made it sound like in opposing the use of land for a new university, we were opposing education. So Studs did give us the chance of making it clear we were not: what we were against was the breaking up of the community.

He took that as his theme for his first book, *Division Street: America,* the breakup of community and the dividing of society. It's some small matter of pleasure to me that for that he interviewed me, and he gave me the number-one position, the speaker of what he calls the "Prologue" to his book.

And he's such a good interviewer—he presses just the right buttons to get you talking. I'm no actress or television personality, I'm just your ordinary person who's not used to being interviewed at all: and how he got me talking to him I don't know, but he did. I was scared at the idea before I did it. You know when he said he was doing this book and wanted to interview me for it, I mean who wouldn't be? What's he going to ask me, am I going to say the right things? But he makes it so easy! It's like when you go to the dentist, and he says "Now this isn't going to hurt"—and it doesn't, and you feel great afterwards. It's just the same with his interviewing.

I talked with some of the other Hull House people he had on his program, and they all said it was the same for them too. He'd talk to them a little beforehand, to make sure he was going to ask them the questions that would let them put over the points they wanted to make. And then as they were doing the studio recording he'd encourage them along, he'd say "Yeah! Yeah! That's great! Just say that again to make sure we've got it good and clear." And then they'd edit his remarks out of it, so you got the person speaking and putting over what they wanted to say in a very compelling manner.

Over the years we still sometimes meet, though I don't go out so much these days on my own since my husband died. But what's remarkable is he won't maybe see me for a year, but as soon as he does he knows who I am instantly. He knows my name, where I come from, where we met last, what we talked about—it's amazing. When you think of all the hundreds and hundreds of people he's meeting and talking with almost every day of the year. And I've never heard of him making a mistake, not one; that's the one story you never hear anyone tell about him.

It must be wearing for his wife, I'm sure, that wherever he goes he always wants to be the center of things. Well, wants to be, I guess he doesn't have much choice, he *is* the center of things. She doesn't have any choice about it and neither does he, and he revels in it. I don't know her very well, she must be a very strong person. What I do know is that whenever I do meet her it's with him and she always comes over as a very sweet person.

And that's a strange thing that I've said, it hadn't struck me that way before you know. When we started to talk I told you I'd known him all my life, or that was how it felt—with a great feeling of warmth, great feeling of affection. But it's true too about him what I've just said about Ida, his wife. I don't really know *him* all that well, either. Strange, that, don't you think, isn't it? There's parts of himself that he keeps so private.

Beverley Podewell, Actress

At seventy-six, her voice was still deep and resonant, her eyes smiling and her manner gracious and at ease. She sat on the settee by the window of her fifth-floor apartment: on the coffee table near it the day's newspaper and two books, one a biography of Henry Irving and the other Gielgud's An Actor in His Time.

—Well I wouldn't say I knew him terribly well darling, but I did have the great pleasure of working with him regularly once a week on TV for two years. I was the waitress in the show called *Studs' Place* which no one has ever forgotten even though it was what feels like a thousand years ago.

It ran like I say two years almost and then suddenly it was dropped without any explanation, though a while afterwards someone with the TV company told me it was because our ratings dropped and we weren't selling enough coffee for our sponsors. Well that may have been true darling or it may not, I wouldn't know. But other folk'll tell you it was for other reasons, political ones. I find that hard to believe because there sure wasn't anything in what we put out that was in any way political—but anyway, we were off air, so there you go.

I'll always remember doing it and what fun it was though, that's something I'll never forget. I'd never done anything like it before, and I've never done anything like it since.

Let me tell you how it went. There was Studs who played the proprietor, there was a blues pianist—a real blues pianist, but in the show he was supposed to be resident there—a guy who had a guitar and was sort of an itinerant, and Grace the waitress, who was me. I didn't play her at any particular age except the one that I was, which was round thirty something as they say these days, and she came from Topeka, Kansas, from a Kansas Quaker family like I do. And such crazy things happened, you wouldn't believe.

The one that sticks in my mind most was a letter, a piece of fan mail I suppose you'd call it. It was from a professor of psychiatry at a university, and you know what? He watched the show, he was hooked on it! And he sent us this letter analyzing all four of us who were the main characters, and what we stood for and what we were symbolic of. And Grace, which was me, I was the "anima"—I think I have the word right—which is the innermost female personality, I was the mother figure who stood for the whole world. I tell you, we all hooted, we really did! And Studs read it out and he said "Well what d'you know, Bev" he said, "I bet you never guessed that that's what you were, now did you?"

That was a high spot, and there were plenty of others—but the thing was, there weren't any low ones, we never did a show which we didn't enjoy and which it seemed like it hadn't come off. It was always so fresh, so new and so different—and that was because we never knew from one week to the next how each show was going to turn out. And *that* was because we were extemporizing, making up our own lines. We had a plot line, a story line such as it was—we were given that at the beginning of the week, and we took it home and mulled it over for a couple of days in our minds and thought through roughly what the characters we were supposed to represent might say about it—and then we met for a couple of days' rehearsal, then the fifth day the camera shot it.

We had the one set, always the same, which was the diner with the piano and the small bar. And there was no director as such, the camera focused on whichever one of us was talking, long shot, medium shot, close up, reaction shots and that was about all it did.

The story line was never any great drama, it was usually some slight, gossamer thing—and it might include some character coming in who was in town that week, and he'd have a small part. He might be a real person, or he might be an invented one. There was never any dialogue given us with the plotline though, not one word—we made that up as we went along.

One episode we did, I remember, was when the Studs character suddenly started talking to the rest of us about classical music and opera and so on. All in a very superior sort of a way, you know, looking down his nose at us as though we were the plebs who couldn't be expected to know about these things. We were all looking at him and at each other, muttering to each other you know, "Where's he got all this stuff from, he doesn't know anything about opera, what's going on?" And then of course a guy comes in and he's from the opera company that's playing in town that week, and somehow Studs had run into him some place and the guy'd given him a couple of freebies for the show the night before.

And Studs has been repeating all the phrases this guy's using now for real, so he collapses like a pricked balloon. It was all stuff of that sort, some slight ordinary thing, sometimes jokey, sometimes serious like I'd had a letter which I wouldn't tell anyone about saying my pa was ill, something like that.

You always felt—*I* always felt, and I know the other three regulars did too—that what we were doing was new, it was innovative, it was exciting, it was something that hadn't been tried before. And it was true, it was all of those things. Yet it was simple and direct, without being what's the word, "homey," you know what I mean? We none of us went in for philosophy, we weren't homespun philosophers, we were ordinary people in an ordinary place doing an ordinary job.

And the thing that glued it all together, the person that kept it that way, undoubtedly, it was Studs. He had this great gift, you know, of finding people exciting, finding life exciting, and it was all around him everywhere, when we were working. His secret was he always wanted to discover, you know? Let me explain a little more about that.

We were at some gathering somewhere, a party or something after one of the shows, the sponsors inviting some of their big-shot customers to have drinks with the cast—something of that sort, I don't remember the details of it. And we were all standing around making conversation in a group with a group of people we didn't know, when one of them said something that was pretty outrageous about something, something I felt very deeply about. Maybe it was religion or politics, I don't know, but it was something that really got to me.

And I started to explode. I shouldn't have done, not in that company and on an occasion of that sort. But I was much younger then, and here was this guy sounding off about oh I don't know what, maybe he was saying slavery was good for black people, it raised their living standards, or something Neanderthal like that. And like I said, the volcano in me just started to erupt.

And Studs said, he said "Now wait a minute Bev, hold it there will you? We all know what you think about this issue, we all know what we all think about this issue. But let's find out what this gentleman thinks, let's ask him to tell us more about what he thinks, and why he thinks it."

You know, that taught me one hell of a lesson it did, and I've never forgotten it the whole of my life. I can't say I've always been one hundred percent perfect in practicing it, but it's been a useful reminder to me about myself, a kind of temperature controller many many times.

No, don't mention it, it's been my pleasure talking to you about him, it truly has.

M. N. Newman, Newspaper Reporter

We sat in the bright morning sunlight at the dining table in his apartment. His wife brought in a neatly laid tray of coffee, with bone-china rose-decorated cups and a cream jug and sugar bowl, and a plate with some homemade cookies on it, and then with a silent smile went back to the kitchen.

—Thanks Nancy. You'll be able to stay and have a bite of lunch with us I hope? You and me'll talk before that, then afterwards Nancy says she'd be glad to talk with you as well if you'd be interested to.

Well now sir, Studs Terkel mm? I should think my acquaintance with him goes back to more than fifty years ago, when I first started out as a young reporter on the *Chicago Sun Times*. I should think I could rightly boast of being one of the few people alive today who can remember his very first broadcasts. Radio wasn't in its infancy but Studs Terkel was as far as being a radio personality's concerned. It was before he ever had his own weekly shows certainly, or was anywhere near established as that. It was the days when he was doing sportswriting, sportscasting, anything and everything so long as it was work.

It wasn't long, though, before they gave him occasional spots—I don't recall exactly, but I think it was usually an hour on a Saturday evening, something like that. The reason I remember them so clear is the same as why I'm sure a lot of other folks do so too—because they were totally different from anything else anyone had thought of doing on radio before.

Are you familiar with an American writer who was popular in the thirties, someone called Damon Runyon? That's right, yeah, he wrote stories about a bunch of New York near-hoods and nobodies and layabouts, and he gave them names like "Harry the Horse" who was a gambler, and stuff like that. They were comic characters. As a matter of fact they're having a revival nowadays because someone's done a successful musical using those same characters of Runyon's, it's called *Guys and Dolls.*

What Studs did was this. Each week he took the story of some well-known opera, and he retold it as a different one of Damon Runyon's characters would tell it. All opera plotlines are pretty stupid if they're just told straight anyhow, but of course when you heard them in that rasping gangster-voice which Studs had—he played gangsters for a time on radio, you know, in soaps—when you heard them retold that way, it was very very funny indeed. Like *The Marriage of Figaro,* you know—"This week I'm gonna tell you about this guy who ran a barber shop in Seville, Spain" or some other near-illiterate telling you the story of *Pagliacci* or *La Bohème*—and of course you didn't know whether to laugh or cry at the mangling of it.

But—and this was what made it so different, and kept you transfixed listening to it—when he came to a big aria or a big duet or chorus, he played you it sung by the really great singers who were famous in those roles—Caruso, Dame Nellie Melba, the chorus of La Scala Opera, Milan—you never knew what you were going to get, but it would be the very best there was. It's hard to convey what the effect of those programs on people was—like I say, it made them laugh *and* it made them cry. And the research he must have put into it, it's unbelievable.

So there was that, and then it wasn't long before they gave him his own regular space. They had to, listeners demanded it. And he just took off. He played jazz, folk music, country music, ballads, everything. He discovered the great gospel singer Mahalia Jackson and introduced her to Chicago—though if you say that, he won't accept it, he always says it was her own black people who discovered Mahalia long before we did. He was among the first to broadcast Burl Ives, and at a guess I'd say there were thousands of people who'd never heard of Beethoven either until they heard him on Studs's show.

Then he did his first book, *Division Street,* and we ran extracts from it in the *Sun Times,* and I went along and interviewed him for a couple of pieces about him that we did to accompany those. And I interviewed him again when he won the Pulitzer for *"The Good War"*—we did a really big piece on him of course that time. He was one of the easiest people to interview I've ever met, because so long as you don't tread on his personal private ground, the man just never stops talking! So much of it is so good too, your biggest problem is what to leave out.

He's interviewed me twice on his radio show, and for that he's the one who gets *you* talking. You're not even thinking about it, you're telling him your views on everything, and he sits there listening, it's terrific what he does and how he does it. And there's this thing he has of making you feel, right from the moment you first meet him, that you're friends. And you *are* friends, whenever you meet thereafter, it's extraordinary, I don't know how he does it, I truly don't.

Here's one odd thing though and I was thinking about it before you came, trying to work out why it should be, but I can't. I've interviewed him for my newspaper, he's interviewed me for his radio show, and over the years we've met and had lunch or a drink together I don't know how many times, so I'd say we got on pretty good. But he's twice tried to interview me for one of his books—and it hasn't worked out either time. I just don't know why that should be. The last one was for this new thing he's published, I believe it's called *Coming of Age* and it's interviews with people over seventy. When he'd done his interview with me for it, we neither of us even had to think about it, we knew straight away it wasn't any good and we agreed to scrap it. And the same thing happened when he interviewed me for a book before, I forget which one, maybe it was *American Dreams.* Maybe he doesn't think of the right questions for me, or he gives me too long to think about my answers and I get tongue-tied or what, I don't know. But it doesn't work, and I wish it did because I'd like that to be part of immortality for me, being in one of Studs Terkel's books.

Oh that's an easy question to answer, which one do I think's the best? *Working,* by a long long way. Because it seems to me that in that one he's gone right into people's hearts and thoughts and feelings in a way nobody else has ever done in a nonfiction way before. People have tried it and done it with individual characters, you feel they've really and truly done it, like say John Steinbeck did in *The Grapes of Wrath*—but that was with one set of people, a small group and maybe in many ways deeper. But what Studs did in *Working* was present us with a panorama of the human race, or the American part of it, in and around the middle of the twentieth century. It has sociological value, it has historical value, it has revelatory value—and above all it has value because it speaks of the human spirit and to the human spirit. And that's some achievement.

Nancy Newman, Public Relations Consultant

—I've known Studs ever since I was a very young woman, from way before when Bill and I were married. It was through my uncle and aunt, whose home was about a block and a half from where Nelson Algren lived, and I don't remember how it was exactly that my uncle knew Algren—but they were both in the newspaper world, so it would be something to do with that, I guess. I used often to go to my uncle's and I met Algren there, and one time Studs was with him.

And as everybody will tell you, Studs always remembers everyone he meets, so that was how it was with us. Sometimes we'd be riding the same bus together on our way home from work. We used to have long long chats together, or at least we did the times Studs wasn't having long chats with everybody else on the bus, or emceeing a debate among all the passengers together. Those bus rides, they were something, I can tell you. And as you know, Studs always still takes the bus into work because he doesn't drive.

One of the great loves of my life in those days—no, *the* great love of my life—was jazz, and we used to talk about that. Then one day he told me with great excitement that a publisher was going to do a book of pieces he'd written about jazz musicians, and it was to be called *Giants of Jazz*. I ordered a copy from a bookstore, and when it was published I took it to him and asked him would he inscribe it for me, which of course he did. He got a kick out of having a fan.

Since those days, Bill and I have got to know him and Ida and we go out to eat together a lot and know each other well. I'd say they're among our closest friends. He may be very famous and all of that—he *is* very famous—but to me and Bill, he and Ida are just ordinary people like the rest of our friends. Being with them is no different in any way to how they are to us or us to them.

The most remarkable aspect of him is this amazing facility he has of picking up a conversation with you at the very point it broke off last time. "Heh Nancy, you know what you were saying about those new apartments going up on Addams Street, well I was thinking about that and the point you were making. . . ." And this was maybe two three weeks before. You find yourself saying to yourself "Oh was I, did I say that? Oh yeah . . ." You have to try and keep your own mind as nimble as his, but you never can.

And all the time there's this kind of effervescent quality he has, where the conversation bubbles along. You think you'd get tired of it, but somehow you don't, it kind of stimulates you too, because he's got such fire in him, especially when he's blasting off about things that he disagrees with. Sometimes I think that's maybe why he and Bill get along together so well: Bill's the quiet thoughtful type who doesn't give his opinion until he's turned something carefully over in his mind, while Studs'll have an instant point of view about something. Maybe it's the same conclusion they both come out with—usually it is, more often than not—and sometimes Studs'll say things because he likes a good argument now and again. But at heart I'd say they're two men who care about the same things—corruption in politics, both at local and state levels, power struggles and the two-facedness of so many of our public figures, the roughshod riding-over of the ordinary man by the big corporations and so on.

Then too there's this big act Studs perpetually puts on about machines. It might be something small like how to work a tape recorder, which is ridiculous when you come to think about it. I mean he uses it to make his living with, when he interviews people for his books, and these days they're so simple even someone like me could learn how to operate one in five minutes, because they're as near as dammit foolproof now. Or he won't—well he's too old now, but he wouldn't—drive a car—because it was a machine. I mean what does he want, going back to everyone riding around on horses? What does he think we should all be—Luddites?

I won't forget one day, ever, when me and Bill were lunching with him and afterwards he asked us to go back with him to his office for some reason or other. You've been to the skyscraper block that WFMT Radio has one floor of, what is it, the eighth or something? Well apparently till the week before, the elevators had had operators, but they'd got rid of them and made them fully automated. So we get this great performance from Studs, we stand in the lobby waiting, and there's no one around and just this line of tight-shut doors. So Studs starts saying "See, there aren't any elevators, that's what you get when there's no guys operating them!" So Bill says "Studs, if you want an elevator you press that button there." "This one?" says Studs, so he presses it and then he says "But you see, nothing happens!" "Wait a minute Studs" says Bill, "now just wait a minute"—and then of course after a second or two, one of the pairs of doors slides open and we all get in. Then what does he do, he stands there looking helpless until Bill leans over in front of him and presses the button for the eighth floor or whatever it was, and as the doors close he makes a big play of nearly having his arm caught between them while they're closing. Up to the eighth we go, and once more he gives us the startled bit as the doors open, and then the play with nearly having his hand trapped as they close again behind us when we get out. And he's shouting "Bring back the men, bring back the men!"

And all of this, you know, this is just one big *act* to entertain us— because you knew damn well if he'd been on his own, none of it would have taken place. Unless, that is, there were other people, strangers, using the elevators too, when they'd have been treated to it.

But then you see in another sense, it's not an act at all. It's Studs's protest, not just at machines taking over our lives, but under the comedy act there's his anger and sadness at the fact there's eight, ten, twelve elevator operators lost their jobs because of it.

He's typecast himself as this jaunty little figure with the red checked shirt ambling along smoking a cigar, when it's winter with his red muffler and his pulled-down porkpie hat, and he always acts up to that image, and wherever he goes in Chicago people recognize him and love him for it. He makes them laugh and he brings them the fun in life, but he brings the world to Chicago, too—on his radio show for years he's given them the world of jazz music and classical music, and books and the people who write them, and painters and dancers and just about everybody from everywhere. And he's given Chicago to the world too, in his books, as well as large parts of the rest of America.

He's a phenomenon, and I hope he goes on forever.

Peggy Terry, Poverty Action Group Worker

We talked in the tiny kitchen at the back of her small bungalow on the outskirts of a nondescript town forty miles to the northwest of Chicago. There were family

photos everywhere, of grown-ups, weddings and children, an Amtrak poster of a
train winding its way through a mountain gorge, and a monthly flower-picture
calendar. She was pale and elderly and in poor health: but when she talked there
was a smile on her face and her voice was soft and warm.

—I haven't seen Studs in five years, but he calls me up once a month
or so to see how I'm getting along, and we talk about our news of our
families, so that way we're regularly in touch. In my time he's interviewed
me for three of his books—*Hard Times, Working* and *"The Good War"*
and maybe he'll interview me for his new one about old people or maybe
not. I tell him if he hasn't got enough material for it, all he has to do's
come over and see me. I've never been on his radio program but I
wouldn't want to be. I'm one of his ordinary people that he builds his
books around, and that's how I like it.

My father was a poor white in the south, and I was born in Kentucky
where he was working as a coal miner. You'll have heard the expression,
my family were what's known in the South as "white trash," and we were
always on the move. As a girl I worked picking cotton in the fields, and
many a time me and my brothers were taken out of class at school to go
and help, so none of us had what could be called any proper sort of an
education. I cut wheat in Kansas, was a supermart checker in Alabama,
and a factory worker in North Carolina.

Like always though, whoever you are and wherever you are, you've
always got to have someone to look down on. In our case it was black
people, or niggers as we always called them. Several of my family were
members of the Ku Klux Klan: my father wasn't, but he was sympathetic
to them. I remember as a child he once took me to a Klan meeting, and
there were all these people there in their pointed hoods and carrying
their burning crosses—and it didn't seem scary, it was something you
were glad that existed, this organization which was always going to up-
hold the supremacy of the whites.

I was married at fifteen, and my husband was seventeen. He finally
gave up on hoping ever to find work that paid a decent wage in the
South, and decided we'd move to Chicago. Our families were against it
very strongly, they said in Chicago the niggers ran everything: but we
thought well we couldn't be no worse off than we were there, so that's
why we came.

I soon found out there was as much prejudice against black people in

Chicago as there was in the South, the only difference being they didn't say it so openly. And the other prejudice Chicago had was almost just as strong, and that was against poor whites. I remember I tried to get a job as an operator with a telephone company, and they turned me down because of my southern accent. They said to my face, they said if one of our customers were to speak on the telephone to you, he'd think he'd gotten a wrong connection and was hooked up with Alabama or somewhere.

My husband did better, he got work at an employment office, then from there he went on to office work in campaign politics with the Democrats. He used to come home at night and say what nice people he worked with, and he said he'd like to bring one of them home to our apartment one night to have a meal with us, a woman who I think was his supervisor, and she was called Emma. I told him OK fine, go ahead—and he said "She's black." I said I wasn't cooking no meal for a black person, and he said he'd had to put up with various drunken members of my family in his time—which was true—and if that was my attitude about a person he worked so well with, just because of the color of her skin, then he and I had better part.

So Emma came for dinner, and after I'd got over the shock of finding myself actually being friendly with a black person, I found her to be one of the nicest people I've ever known. We got to know each other well, she came many evenings to eat with us, and we went to her home for meals with her—and in due course she got me interested in the political work she did, which was campaigning on behalf of minorities—all minorities, the poor, the underprivileged, whether they were black *or* white, the Amero-Indians, single mothers—all those who need help and who the last thing on earth that mattered was the color of their skin.

It was she who took me one night to meet the man who often joined with them in their work, not by making speeches but by sitting on organizational committees and getting things done. And that man's name was the Reverend King, whom I came to know long before he was a national figure, and who I thought was one of the kindest politest gentlemen I've ever met. I've sat round tables with him and ten twelve other people all working towards the same end, and he listened to what everyone else said and added in his opinion when it was his turn, but never once did he try and take it over himself. A wonderful man, and when they killed him, we Americans I can tell you, we killed half of our soul.

I've often thought and I've wondered how it could come about that someone like me who came from such a racist background and family like I did, could so completely change. If I knew what it was, I can tell you, I'd bottle it and spread it around. It was such a change in my whole life's attitude, and I think what crystalized it for me was going to one of our meetings one night and seeing Reverend King come in bruised and bleeding after he'd been beaten up in the street by a gang of white youths just because he was black—and hearing the way he spoke about it, his gentle forgiving attitude, and the way he had no hate for anyone, anywhere in his heart.

But all that's a different matter though isn't it to the one you've come to talk to me about, which is how I came to know Studs? I met him years later, for the first time, on the Peace Train, when I was going to Washington with Emma to the big rally, which the Reverend King who was by then a famous figure was going to address. Studs was on that train talking to people, and Emma knew him and she introduced us. We had a long conversation together, and that's how we came to be friends.

Studs hadn't done any of his books yet at that time, but when he was preparing his second one, which I think was *Hard Times* about the Depression, he remembered me and interviewed me and my mother, and then like I said he interviewed me for some of his later ones. He was always so easy to talk to, it didn't matter who you were or where. I remember once he did one of his interviews with me in a crowded room full of people after some meeting or other that we'd both been present at. He found a couple of chairs and we sat on our own in a corner somewhere, and he asked me help him fix his tape recorder so that it worked properly, I remember, and then we just talked. Or I should say it was me that talked, he just asked me a question a time or two, that was all. And it didn't matter that all these other people were there moving around chattering with each other—he made you feel you were the only one there who mattered to him, which of course while you were talking to him, you were.

I'd say that he's just himself with everybody, and that's what makes him so special. I listen in to his radio program sometimes, and I don't hear any difference in the way he talks to somebody famous and the way when we're on the telephone he talks to me. And when in his books he talks to people like me, well the only way I can put it is to say that he gives a voice to the voiceless, that's what he does.

4

Getting It Together

Sir Georg Solti
Dr. Oliver Sacks

These extracts from two contrasting radio interviews show the difference between a poor interview and a good one.

In the first, with the mercurial and volatile Sir Georg Solti, the ill-prepared Studs soon found himself at a loss. His control slid away: the interview degenerated into interruptions, misunderstandings, contradictions, staccatos, and repetitions which were the verbal equivalents of what is known in television as "reaction shots."

With Dr. Oliver Sacks, on the other hand, the interview flowed smoothly, with the speakers sparking ideas off each other and forgetting their studio surroundings.

Interview with Sir Georg Solti

(Opening music for 2¹/₂ minutes)

Studs: That was part of Mozart's overture to *The Magic Flute,* recorded
by the Chicago Symphony Orchestra conducted by its musical
director laureate, Sir Georg Solti,* who is here with me today.
And well, Sir George, I suppose the first thing we should say to
each other isn't it, is that we were both born in 1912 so we're
both the same age?

Solti: Yes, but are looking much younger I hope.

Studs: And your artistry of course becomes more and more rich.

Solti: You can say that is the case, but I cannot say it for myself. But in
some ways the calendar works in our favor. I am mentally
stronger but physically weaker, it is only natural.

Studs: So how did you begin? You studied with Bartók I believe?

Solti: And with Dohnányi.

Studs: And with Dohnányi, and—

Solti: And with Kodály also.

Studs: And with Kod—

Solti: But of course you see it began much sooner than that, because I

---

* Pronouncing it phonetically and correctly as "Sir George Sholti"

went to a very good school. In Budapest. Have you ever been to Budapest?

Studs: No, I—

Solti: It is very beautiful city. And in Hungary we had very good educational system. I am education fanatic. I firmly believe that education is absolutely essential, and it fills me with sadness that in the United States musical education has been struck out from your schools and you do not give money to it. It is a great mistake because for musical education there should be money always. Art is what makes a nation. If it is comprised of educated people that nation will flourish, but badly educated people have no future. You have some wonderful universities, probably the best in the world, but the link is missing.

Studs: What link, how do you mean?

Solti: Middle school—the school between ten and eighteen.

Studs: Ah, I—

Solti: You call it high school, we call it gymnasium or whatever, but it is the same. This is where you form human beings, and it is not very good here.

Studs: So in your formative years as you say, you were in Budapest?

Solti: My musical education could not have been better. I was good pupil and fairly industrious—but at music only, I was not talented at other things. There was tremendous competition to get into the high school for music, and you would either survive or you would die. I survived because I am tough. But many died, I mean in the spiritual sense.

Studs: We hear the word "competition" a great deal today, but you mean with within yourself?

Solti: Yes, you had to go twice a week with five or six others to piano lessons.

Studs: Uh-huh and—

Solti: And you also played the same material.

Studs: Yes and—

Solti: And so you had to concentrate very much.

Studs: So you learned first the piano and not to conduct. Now tell me about Bartók. I've heard he was a very outwardly cool person but very passionate inside.

Solti: Shy, not cool, no, very shy. I didn't know him well, I must discourage that legend. He did not teach composition, he taught piano, and when I was about fifteen or sixteen he took our piano classes. And by the way I went there to the school when I was there recently, and visited all the classrooms.

Studs: Recently?

Solti: Three years ago.

Studs: Oh, three years ago?

Solti: It was very interesting. And nostalgic.

Studs: Yes it must have—

Solti: Nothing had changed, everything was exactly the same as I remembered it. Except the pianos, I suppose they had replaced those.

Studs: Oh. Yes.

Solti: And so we played for him.

Studs: For Bartók.

Solti: Yes. Very stupidly I myself once I myself brought one piece to play for him which was by him. And he did not want to hear it. He said "No no play something else"

Studs: Oh.

Solti: And so I played Bach, I played Mozart. He loved Debussy, he loved Scarlatti, he loved Liszt. Not the heavy German romantics.

Studs: Not?

Solti: No. He did not play Beethoven and Brahms, he played a great deal of Bach, Scarlatti and Liszt. And Debussy. Debussy was one of his favorite composers.

Studs: He was?

Solti: He played Debussy very often to us. It was first of all very frightening to us, you can imagine. When you go to a class—

Studs: It was frightening?

Solti: I adored him, I worshiped him, so when you are as near as I am now to you it is very frightening. He spoke very softly like this. And he said very little.

Studs: He said very little?

Solti: When I am finished playing a piece, he would say "Listen to this" and then sit down and play it to show it, or he would make a few comments and say "Bring it again next week. I want to hear it again next week. Work on this and this and this, and bring it again next week." And with time we lost our fears be-

	cause he was very nice. Very gentle but it was always a tremendous distance you see.
Studs:	Distance?
Solti:	Yes distance always. And I then saw him once or twice after that because I became a repetiteur.
Studs:	A repetiteur?
Solti:	A repetiteur is in an opera house a man playing a piano and working with the singers before the conductor comes in to them.
Studs:	He warms them up?
Solti:	No, he works with them. This was when I was eighteen. And I remember I worked with the conductor and we performed a ballet which was considered very scandalous at that time, but it was not scandalous at all. It was called *The Miraculous Mandarin*.
Studs:	Oh yes, *The Miraculous Mandarin*, I—
Solti:	But because we lived in a fascist state—
Studs:	Under Horthy—
Solti:	It was considered immoral and written by a communist, so he emigrated to Russia and we only played it once. But I never forgot seeing him at the rehearsal, he took a metronome from his pocket—you know what a metronome is?
Studs:	Yes it's—
Solti:	It is for measuring the speed of the beat. He was very precise with his metronome and corrected the conductor—"That was too fast, that was too slow" he was meticulous about his tempo, but all very gentle.

.   .   .

Solti:	And in the war I was in Switzerland, but I don't want to talk much about that period because we do not have the time to tell my whole life. And also I intend to write my autobiography this year.
Studs:	Oh that'll be great.
Solti:	Because I am the only living musician today who went through two world wars. There is nobody else.
Studs:	Yes all right.
Solti:	After the war I went to the opera house in Budapest, but I was thrown out because of the anti-Jewish legislation.
Studs:	You were seventeen?
Solti:	No I was twenty-five, this was in 1937. The director of the opera

house said to me "But I am not worrying about you, you are so talented that you will make your way anyway." So I was out on the street. And I met a friend, and he said to me "Solti, what are you going to do?" and I said "I do not know" and he said "You must go to Lucerne, because Toscanini is there, he has left Italy to escape Mussolini." But I told him I could not go for two reasons. One, that I had no money; and two that I am a coffee-house Hungarian, if you know what I mean.

Studs: *(Laughs)*

Solti: I liked to sit and talk and I liked reading newspapers, I started newspaper reading at thirteen, I really look at newspapers every morning. I still get here two newspapers, I read them every morning. I learned my English from newspapers, if you can call it English, so anyway I went to Lucerne and I spoke to Toscanini and he said to me "All right, come to America and we will try to help you." I thought it would be easy to come to America, but it was quite impossible because the Hungarian quota was filled for fifty years.

Studs: Oh boy.

Solti: So I was stuck but fortunately it was in Switzerland. And then I got a cable from my mother and it said "Don't come home."

Studs: Oh boy.

Solti: But you must understand that in 1939 the people including my-self did not take too seriously the war threat because in the year before there had been the famous Munich pact with Hitler and Chamberlain for peace in our time.

Studs: Peace in our time, yeah.

Solti: And the French began to withdraw from the alliance and there was an article by Monsieur Laval—does it mean anything to you, the name "Laval"?

Studs: Yes, the collaborationist at Vichy and—

Solti: So I was stuck there in Switzerland and could not do anything except play the piano and in 1942 I won the first prize in the Geneva Competition and this kept me alive so to speak. Little money from little engagements.

Studs: All in Switzerland.

Solti: All in Switzerland. And in 1946 I left Switzerland and I started to conduct.

Studs: Aha!

Solti: I was thirty-three years old and I never had any proper opera repertoire.

Studs: And you conducted—

Solti: Very little. Minimum. And so I went to Germany, and from there my life began to move up. I came to Munich through an American friend. We had studied music together, and he was an officer. In Munich there was not one house intact, I had never seen anything like it.

Studs: Who were you conducting for?

Solti: For Americans, American soldiers and Germans. I was there with my wife, who unfortunately died about fifteen years ago, and we lived on cigarettes—selling cigarettes, exchanging them for food, and opera tickets.

Studs: They were that valuable. And you conducted for—

Solti: The Bavarian Opera Company.

Studs: So then you were set as a conductor.

Solti: I worked like a lunatic. I had to acquire a repertoire. So I worked like a madman. I did it well, after six years I had a repertoire of thirty-five to forty operas and then I went to Frankfurt because in Munich there was a mood against me, because the Culture Minister was a Catholic and he wanted a Catholic conductor. So in Frankfurt I spent happy years as musical director at the opera, and I was then invited to conduct in London.

Studs: You introduced new works into the repertoire?

Solti: In London at Covent Garden I conducted *Der Rosenkavalier*. It was such a success. Also the *Ring*—Wagner.

Studs: The complete *Ring*?

Solti: I was ten years in London, it was a very good time, a very happy time. I became a sort of English legend. Then I guest conducted in America, in many places and here in Chicago, and I thought "This is a wonderful orchestra." It was love at the first sight you know.

Studs: You and the Chicago Symphony Orchestra.

Solti: And then I went home and said to my agent "Look, I am tired from this guest conducting, here a week, there a week. Can you make for me a little season in Chicago?" So they said they wanted me as musical director, which now I have been for twenty-two years.

Studs: Twenty-two years . . . What was it about the Chicago Symphony that you saw when you first came?

Solti: That we have the same approach. Namely we are terribly serious about making music. They take it very seriously, they are working very hard. I don't know any other orchestra in the world that works so hard at their practicing. Europeans do not do so much.

Studs: Oh explain that. They don't—

Solti: They don't work as hard as their American counterparts. They have a certain amount of—if you want—arrogance.

Studs: Arrogance?

Solti: They know the music, why should they practice too much? Everybody tries to be working less and less, get away as quick as you can and don't work. But the Americans are taking home their parts and practicing, the musicians are working harder than ever before. It is heartwarming.

.   .   .

Studs: With your wide repertoire of—

Solti: My repertoire is enormous—

Studs: Of operas and symphonies—

Solti: Enormous—

Studs: Endless, you think there are many good new composers?

Solti: Well many composers at first had a rough time, even Beethoven, they said he was crazy, cuckoo. Wagner, Bruckner, Mahler—all had a terrible time, all of them. Mozart.

Studs: Hm?

Solti: Not as a piano player, they saw the wonderful piano player but as a composer.

Studs: So where are we now?

Solti: I don't know where we are. I do not dare to give prognosis because this is foolish and wrong, and I hate to be wrong. There's no way to judge what will happen in twenty years' time. There is not as much productivity of music, so which way the composers will go, it is very difficult, we are in a strange no-light situation. Many avenues can open including technically.

Studs: Oh, yeah. But there have to be other elements, for instance a brain cannot be replaced.

Solti: No it cannot be replaced.

Studs: Or imagination.

Solti: No that cannot be replaced.

Studs: It cannot be.

Solti: No.*

Interview with Dr. Oliver Sacks

Sacks: "I am writing this with my left hand, although I am strongly right-handed. I had surgery to my right shoulder a month ago and am not permitted, not capable of, use of the right arm at this time. I write slowly, awkwardly—but more easily, more naturally, with each passing day. I am adapting, learning, all the while—not merely this left-handed writing, but a dozen other left-handed skills as well."

Studs: Dr. Oliver Sacks, reading from the deceptively casual preface to his most recent book *An Anthropologist on Mars,* which has as its subtitle *Seven Paradoxical Tales.* Oliver Sacks, who has the wonder of a neurologist, the soul of a poet, and the writing skills of a fine novelist. That opening, Oliver, tells me a lot about you and why you are so remarkable in your reaching out to those who are your patients. You speak of your own experience as something that could be a handicap, becoming a new avenue, a new opening for you.

Sacks: Well when I first found my arm immobilized I was in deep trouble, because I'm so strongly right-handed that my balance was off, and I was intrigued at how quickly things started to change. My nervous system was challenged in a way that it had never been before.

* It must in all fairness be recorded that several other interviews with Sir Georg which Studs has conducted, both before and since this one, have been highly successful.

Studs: Is it fair to say that as you talked together, you and your patients, you revealed some of your own vulnerability—that you were almost, as it were, fellow passengers?

Sacks: Yes. Originally I used to think of myself as remote and detached, almost as a sort of godlike figure. But now I feel I'm quite as vulnerable as they are, and there's certainly a feeling of sharing.

Studs: Let's start with your first tale, "The Color-Blind Painter."

Sacks: Well I got a letter from him at the beginning of 1986 saying he had had a head injury in a car accident. He had been stunned and briefly amnesiac, and he had lost all his sense of color, and now saw everything as gray. Since color was so important to him, his paintings were drained of meaning. He found his memory and his imagination had been voided of color too. And he asked me could I help him?

Studs: And what happened?

Sacks: Well when I saw him he was very depressed, and he felt this was the end of him as an artist and as a man. Neurologically the matter was relatively simple. I tested him and it became evident two small areas at the back of the brain had been knocked out, and one needs these areas to construct color. And in that case you can no longer see it or imagine it or remember it or dream it.

Studs: So darkness in a sense becomes light to him—or am I wrong about that?

Sacks: Something like that happened. I couldn't do anything to promote recovery, but I hoped he might slowly feel he could cope with this black-and-white world. Then something dramatic happened—one morning he saw the sunrise, and as he said, it looked apocalyptic, like some huge nuclear explosion, and he wondered if anyone had ever seen the sunrise like that before, and so he painted it—there is a reproduction of it in the book— and he called it *Nuclear Sunrise*—and that for him was the beginning of change, of a new sort of sensibility. And he started to feel that he hadn't just lost something, but that something new and important had come into his life.

Studs: He saw light in a new light? It makes me think of Edward Hopper, I don't know why.

Sacks: Yes and interestingly I know of another totally color-blind person who loves Hopper's work more than anyone else's.

Studs: Why is that?

Sacks: A lot of Hopper's paintings are night scenes.

Studs: *Nighthawks*! Of course!

Sacks: Right, yes! However, to continue with the painter's story—some years later a colleague suggested that it might be possible to try and train another part of his brain to construct color, and when this was suggested to him his response was this—he said "If you had offered this to me at first I would have loved you, because you would have given me back what I had lost. But now I don't want it, color has become meaningless. My world is reconstructed, and it is coherent, and it is fine as it is."

·   ·   ·

Studs: Well now let's pass on to what you call "The Surgeon's Story"— this is the story of a surgeon who had what is known as Tourette's syndrome. Will you explain for those of us who don't know, what Tourette's is?

Sacks: Yes, it involves tics of various sorts—all sorts of convulsive movements and noises, and sometimes thoughts as well, and people who have it seem often what I can only describe as "accelerated" as well. I had met this man at a meeting in Boston, and some of his tics were very extraordinary. One of them consisted of him suddenly putting his foot on top of people's heads. It was a very agile and, one somehow felt, a very affectionate tic. When he told me he was a surgeon and a teacher I couldn't believe it. But when I visited him in Canada I saw him lecturing, and he was lying on his back kicking his foot in the air and at the same time giving a perfectly composed discourse. And when he worked as a surgeon, all his tics disappeared. I scrubbed with him for a long operation which lasted for two and a half hours, and there was no hint of Tourette's while he was doing it. He wasn't controlling it, it was just that there was no impulse to tic at that time because his whole mind was concentrating on what he was doing, thinking of the operation he was performing. One can see this also with Tourettic artists, musicians for instance.

Studs: Wasn't there a jazz drummer who was like that?

Sacks: Yes, he was a famous and very good jazz drummer. And he might suddenly convulsively hit the drums, and then very rapidly improvise on it, and the improvisation was actually partly Tourettic. And when he was on medication to dampen things down, he lost the ability to improvise or even to play decently. So there can be a creative aspect to Tourette's, because it has an energy of its own. Oh and I should mention that it can be focused in a very positive way not only in work, as the surgeon did, but also in the fact that he flew a plane. After I'd seen him I had thought I was going to take a commercial flight back to Calgary, but he said he'd fly me in his own plane. He smiled and said "I'm the only flying Tourettic surgeon in the world," and I was quite taken aback and a little alarmed. I had fantasies that he would spin the plane or loop the loop or he would suddenly leap out, but none of that happened and in fact he was a superb pilot just as he was a superb surgeon.

.   .   .

Studs: And now we come to autism—and "autism" immediately is a frightening word, as it is a frightening burden we know, to young people and to others. Let's start with the young kid Stephen Wiltshire the artist whom you describe, some of whose drawings are reproduced in your book.

Sacks: I first came across him when a publisher sent me some examples of his work and some history of him. I was staggered by these exquisite drawings of London, and when I was next there spoke to my brother who is a physician there. He laughed and he said "Stephen? He's a patient of mine." And he told me a little of his early history, that from the age of two Stephen had been manifestly autistic, rocking and screaming, and was sent to a special school where he was regarded as ineducable. But one day when he was six a teacher discovered him doing exquisite tiny drawings of the Tower of London and the Houses of Parliament—but Stephen hadn't gone through any of the usual stages of doodlings and drawings like other children do. By the time I heard about him Stephen had become nationally famous in England, there had been a television program about him and he was about to have a book published. He was a prodigy, with a so-called "savant" gift for drawing, and yet autistic and retarded. I was very curious to meet him, and got the chance to do so the following year when he came to New York. His language was very poor, he would nod his head and smile, but he had only a few words. We went to my home, and he glanced at the outside of it, and then did a beautiful little drawing of it. Actually I think he could have drawn the entire street, because in that single indifferent but comprehensive glance he'd taken it all in. It was puzzling that on the one hand there was this tremendous amount of concentration, while on the other he was whistling and looking around and listening to a tape recorder, so it was only a part of him that was doing the drawing and the rest of him was unconnected. Incidentally I know of another autistic artist, who became a great menace as a forger. He is now employed in one of the great auction houses because he is very good at spotting other people's forgeries!

Studs: Really? So a creative artist can go two ways—can do well and can't do people good, or can do people good.

Sacks: Absolutely. And Stephen seems able to catch anything, whether it's a copy of a Matisse, or a drawing of a cathedral, or a drawing of an elephant. His work is brilliant and it's brought joy to millions of people. A good number of autistic people have great gifts and concentrations—sometimes visual, sometimes musical—and they seem to be unconnected with personality, or the mind as a whole.

Studs: Strengths that come through as a result of the disease. What is it you quote as an epigraph attributed to William Osler at the beginning of your book? "Ask not what disease the person has, but rather what person the disease has."

Sacks: Yes it's always this conjunction. How much has autism brought to Stephen, and how much has Stephen brought to autism?

Studs: There are several such themes in your book—seven in all—and after the break we'll talk about the remarkable woman who gives it its title, *An Anthropologist on Mars*. We are finding out more and more about this crazy thing called "the human condition," and the possibilities there are within which are the things we term "diseases."

Sacks: And the different ways in which people can make their worlds, and how—paradoxically—disease can almost force one to make another and different sort of world.

Studs: And so we'll take our break.

. . .

Studs: We're talking with Dr. Oliver Sacks, and Oliver you were going to tell us about the woman who gave you the title for your new book *An Anthropologist on Mars*.

Sacks: At the age of three she was screaming and rocking and seemed as autistic as Stephen. But then, partly because she had a different form of autism, she was able to acquire good language and all sorts of other intellectual skills, and indeed she is now a professor of animal behavior at a university and, among other things, acknowledged as one of the world's leading experts on cattle psychology. She understands them and loves them deeply, and it was very very moving to see her with cattle, with which she has a tremendous rapport. By contrast, she is totally bewildered by human beings. She finds us opaque, bizarre, dissembling and complicated. She has learned various forms of social behavior by rote, and she says she is studying us closely. It was while she was telling me this that she used the phrase, she said she felt like an anthropologist on Mars.

Studs: On an alien planet?

Sacks: Exactly. Amongst other things she is a very good judge of scientific papers, because she is never swayed by hostility or rivalry. She has a great single-mindedness and honesty and extreme clarity of mind.

Studs: What are her feelings about emotions—love and sex and so on, are they there?

Sacks: I think she sometimes yearns for a relationship. When she was a girl she was very puzzled by "dating"—she didn't know what was expected and what was implied and how she should respond. It became too much for her so she decided to be a scientist and to be celibate. And she has now invented a hug machine.

Studs: A hug machine?

Sacks: She sometimes longs to be hugged, but has always been terrified of physical contact, so she invented this machine that can administer a hug but be controlled by her. It is made from what is called a squeeze-chute for restraining calves when they are examined, and she developed it for herself and she demonstrated its use to me. I was a little embarrassed to be invited into her bedroom to see it, but she herself showed no diffidence and no embarrassment whatsoever. I think these are emotions which are quite unknown to her. And when she lay down in it to demonstrate it, by the same token there was no exhibitionism and no shame. These are the things which she finds so complicated and incomprehensible in us, because of her own lack of them. I remember her saying once "If I could flick my fingers and be nonautistic, I wouldn't—because autism is part of the way I am." And I've met other autistic people who appear almost to take pride in being of another species, rather than being seen as some kind of disabled version of us.

Studs: Is it the work that becomes the key?

Sacks: Well certainly she seems to work work work all the while, and she loves her work, so I think the Freudian prescription of work and love was true of her.

Studs: *"Lieben und Arbeit"*?

Sacks: Right.

Studs: And you write also of something coming out of disorder?

Sacks: Well, right at the end of my visit to her she got into a remarkable state of mind as we were driving to the airport. She started speaking of herself, and said she had been brought up religious, but she'd given up belief in a personal God or agency. I think this may have been partly because of her autism. But she said she had a scientific notion of God as a sort of evolution of order out of disorder in the universe, and she went on to say other people could transmit genes but she couldn't—and she wished she could transmit instead some thoughts and some words. Nietzsche once said the world was a work of art that was creating itself, and I think this notion is something she had strongly.

Studs: Read for us the last paragraph of your book, because it so beautifully sums this up.

Sacks: "As we parked the car and got out, she suddenly faltered and wept. 'I've read that libraries are where immortalities lie' she said. 'I don't want my thoughts to die with me, I want to have done something. I'm not interested in power or piles of money.

I want to leave something behind. I want to make a positive contribution—know that my life has meaning. Right now, I'm talking about things at the very core of my existence.' I was stunned. As we said goodbye, I said 'I'm going to hug you. I hope you don't mind.' I hugged her—and (I think)—she hugged me back.''

5

An Accretion of
Accidents:
Studs Talking (2)

—That's how it's always seemed to me you know—all through my life, one thing's come along, then another, then another—and they've scarcely been in any way connected, some of them were downright fortuitous you might say. An accretion of accidents, that's what they were, that's the way I'd describe it, me being in the right place at the right time. Or sure yeah, that's right, sometimes being in the wrong place at the wrong time. Opening my mouth when it'd've been better if I'd kept it shut and stayed clammed up, yeah.

Born May 1912, I told you that didn't I? When folk ask me I say "Born one month after the *Titanic* sank, I came up when she'd gone down." Maybe it'd have been better the other way round, the ship'd stayed floating and I didn't surface heh?

The Bronx as a small kid, I ought to have remembered more about that shouldn't I? I thought about it last time after we talked, I thought I ought to have remembered more. Only all my memories of growing up as a young kid, even if they're none too happy, they were all of Chicago. Isn't that odd? I wonder why? The selective process of memory, we talked about that didn't we? That must be it. One thing I did remember though was while we were living in Chicago, I came back to New York one time for a short period, maybe only as long as one school semester that's all, and I came back with my mother. It was just her and me, and what we'd come for I don't know—maybe she'd come to see some relative of hers or something, or maybe to sew up some things we'd left behind. Maybe to get some financial help of some sort, I don't know. But you know what? Thinking about it, I remember it was a happy time we had to-gether. That one time was a happy time. I remember with my mother, the only one. So why would that be—because she wasn't with my father and there wasn't the friction between them all the time? Or she didn't have the responsibility of him and three children to look after as well on top of everything, so she felt she could breathe a little? There weren't any special incidents with her in New York I recall, just that it was a short but happy time.

A big jump chronologically now—about the only other time I had a special feeling of happiness when I was young was one time when I was in Chicago around the age of seventeen. For some reason—I think every-one had gone off to a family wedding some place for a couple of days—I was left in sole charge of the rooming house we ran. No, wait a minute my brothers would have moved away because they married by then, so it'd be just my ma and pa who went away. And oh boy, was I proud—the manager of a downtown Chicago rooming house, even if it was only a couple of nights! The monarch of all I surveyed—fifty-two doors, every one of them shut of course, and what was going on behind them nothing to do with me. But what a position, what power! It was great just to sit at the desk in the lobby and see all the comings-in and the goings-out, and have all the just-a-few-word conversations you had. "Good evening Mr. Jacobson, how are you tonight?" "Oh just fine Louis thank you Louis, just fine." "Good, I'm glad to hear that Mr. Jacobson, here's your key." Then the next one "Say, how's it going, Louis?" "Good, thank you Mr. Miller, room twenty-seven isn't it? Here's your key." Funny thing . . . those little informalities, those split-second observations of people—whether they looked in good health or bad health or, more likely, whether they looked like they'd had too much to drink or not, or if they'd had a good day with the horses or a bad one. . . . Heh now, here's a thought, maybe that's what stayed in my mind all that time afterwards when I was being so bored with law school. Maybe without me knowing it, it kept it in my mind that if I did something else, I wanted it to be talking with people, and that's what led me into reporting and journalism and all that stuff.

I don't have a sure idea of the order it all happened in. I did some sports reporting and broadcasting, then I did some newscasting in a small way, and the spare-time radio bit-part acting I told you about. I was much happier doing all of that, even if I wasn't making any great money out of it. I guess I'd say at that time I was a real kaleidoscope sort of a figure, a jack of all this-that-and-the-other. I was an entertainer and an informer and I liked that.

I was in the army for a year in 1942, working for them as a radio newscaster. I'd like to have done more and gone into the Red Cross, but I was in the Reserve, I couldn't go abroad because of my physical-fitness limitation. That was my perforated eardrums because of my childhood mastoiditis operations. I did some political broadcasts for FDR during his campaign for a fourth term as president in 1944—I was always a supporter of him, right from the time he was elected in 1932. Then after the army I got a break—my own radio show. It was called *The Wax Museum*, and what it was was I played mostly jazz records, mostly commercial ones that were available in record stores, but every here and there I slipped in ones which weren't available any more. I used to comb around market stalls and places like that and I got a big kick out of when I found one. Or listeners'd write in and say had I heard about some jazz player and I'd go out looking for his records and listen to them and if I liked them, play them. It was a two-way thing between me and the listeners and it got to be very popular.

Then there came the early days of television and I had a regular show on that called *Studs' Place*. This was supposed to be a small café, with the same basic characters—I was the manager, there was a waitress and a pianist and so on, four of us, and we never changed: but each week different people dropped in. We had a couple of days' rehearsal, sketched out a rough plotline for what we were all going to talk about, then we'd extemporize the dialogue.

It was very relaxed, very casual, very laid back. It played a big part in the development of what was to become known as "Chicago-Style TV." Only then one day out of the blue, whack, the station pulled the program out of the schedules, and it was never seen or heard of again. Why? Because this was 1953, that's why. And what was 1953? Nineteen fifty-three was the era of Senator Joseph McCarthy, and I was one of hundreds, maybe thousands, suspected of being guilty of "un-American activities." Not "guilty," because no charges were made—but "suspected of *being* guilty." I guess it's hard—no, not hard, impossible—for someone who wasn't around in America at that time, to imagine just how things were. It wasn't only that no one would risk employing you if you were suspected of un-American activities, it was far worse than that. No one would employ anyone who *employed* anyone who was suspected of un-American activities. It took right up until McCarthy so far overreached himself as to accuse President Eisenhower, a Republican, of being soft on communism that even the Republicans themselves had had enough, and turned their backs on him.

So that brought the end of *Studs' Place,* and when it got around why—that it was because of me, that affected people's readiness to offer me any work, either for the radio or any other kind. Not because they were scared it'd be un-American, or that I was—they knew I wasn't—but they were afraid what'd happen to *them* if they gave me work. It was a tough time financially, real tough. I always say I guess the only benefit I got from it was it gave me lots of spare time to read, and research some of my favorite subjects, such as jazz which I was in the end able to make use of when I did my book *Giants.*

It took a year or so after McCarthy for me to get back into regular work. It happened, but very gradually. I did some disc-jockey-type programs at WFMT—and then I got another break again, I was offered a spot on a weekly basis. Then on a daily basis—and forty years later, that's where I still am now. How lucky can you get? It's my bread and butter and it always has been. I love it. Whether the others who're responsible for recording it in the studio, and cutting it and editing it, and putting it out, as well as all the arranging and administration that goes along with it—well, I guess they'll tell you whether *they* love it or not, that's if they haven't already done so.

It goes out an hour each day, five days a week. Most times it's a new item, an interview, but sometimes it's a repeat. We put out a feature program once a year, on the anniversary of the day they dropped the bomb on Hiroshima. It's called "Born to Live," and it's a documentary I did with Jim Unrath. We made it as a montage of voices—Japanese recalling what they were doing when they were schoolchildren that day, Americans, Pete Seeger singing a ballad, actors reading poems, a mother teaching her child how to talk by saying to it "Happy—happy—happy" and the child repeating it back "Ha-ppy ha-ppy ha-ppy." It was good to do, and it's good to remind people once a year of Hiroshima with it. It won the Prix Italia, which is the big prize they give for radio work.* Or another anniversary one we have is called "This Train": it's interviews I

* The cassette of this is issued by the Smithsonian Institution, Washington, D.C.

recorded the day the Peace Train went from here to Washington taking people to hear Martin Luther King speak at a big rally, and on the way I asked them what their hopes for the day were, and on the way back again their feelings about the way it'd gone.

There's another repeat we do every year which'll be going out this Friday, which is J. S. Bach's birthday. We'll have some of his music, maybe one of the *Brandenburg* Concertos, part of a violin concerto, and also a couple of little novelties in it which people don't hear too often— say like "Air on a G String" but played on a banjo, or "Jesu Joy of Man's Desiring" but played by someone on an ocarina. Oh yeah, and we read out a list of twenty Christian names too. You know what they are? The Christian names of the twenty children that he had! This one's a very popular program, we get listeners writing in weeks ahead, they say "I'm just reminding you it's Bach's birthday coming up next month, you *are* going to do your program about him again aren't you?"

But like I say, it's not mostly repeats, it's mostly interviews. Someone's in town I've talked to before, so I have them in to tell how they're getting along. Or a writer's got a new book out, and I invite them to come and talk about it. The thing I don't like to do is the usual type of conventional arts program, you know what I mean? A bunch of critics sounding off about something, all giving their opinions and trying to outsmart each other. I want to put things over a bit differently if I can find a way of doing it.

There was one a few months back, I timed it so's it would coincide with a retrospective exhibition of Edward Hopper's paintings at the Chicago Arts Institute. Instead of just talking about them, we had short pieces of music that people said his works reminded them of, then in between we put readings of what people had written about it in the past. Things like Stuart Dybeck's piece called "Killing Time," about how whenever he wandered around the gallery he always seemed to end up in front of Hopper's *Nighthawks*—then further on in, we had someone read Joyce Carol Oates' description of the same painting, which she wrote six years ago. Some more music, then some vox pops we recorded in the gallery of folk who'd never been in there before, strangers from out of town. "What do you think of this guy's stuff, why'd you like it, which ones do you particularly like? You sir, what do you think, you don't like it, tell us why you don't like it." Made quite a lively program, because it wasn't just about paintings, it was about paintings and music and people, a different sort of an arts program to the kind you usually hear.

Another thing we do is one part of a program live, and one part repeat. I put in a recording of Eleanor Bron reading something like let's say a part of *Madame Bovary* she once did: or a story by Nelson Algren. I repeat them because I like them, or I've had requests for them. There's some people say—I say it myself sometimes—radio's ephemeral, it doesn't last—but in that kind of way it does, it stays in people's minds. If they want to hear something again, most times we can find it in our tape library and play it for them.

There's a satisfaction, to be able to do something like that. To be an entertainer, to be an informer, to be able to present people with something they enjoy hearing—even if you're not actually the one who's doing it yourself. Is that a kind of childishness, to satisfy someone's request? "You want to hear Widor's Toccata and Fugue played on the organ of Chartres Cathedral? OK, I have that for you here, sit back and listen. You want to hear the voice of Caruso, so you can decide for yourself whether he was all he was cracked up to be? OK OK, no problem, we have an example for you. Bessie Smith? Fine! Maria Callas? Coming up!" You get a good feeling, out of something just as simple as that. Makes you feel you're loved. Is that crazy?

Heh, maybe we're getting to too deep water here, maybe this isn't the time and the place. Let's touch that button again another time, and see what comes out.

You feel like some lunch? What'll it be today, Italian or Chinese?

.   .   .

—You know, I was thinking. Thinking about my mother again, while we were walking back. Odd the way thoughts of her come floating into my mind for no reason. It's not because I see something or hear something that reminds me of her, it's nothing like that. I'm not conscious of thinking about *anything*, and then I find I *am* thinking, just in a generalized kind of a way, you know what I mean, and it's about *her*. I was thinking as we were walking that nearly always—nearly always that I remember, anyhow—that you know how I told you folk were always kind of bracing themselves for what she might say? Well now here's the funny thing: that it *was* nearly always that I can remember that the person she'd attack and slam into was a man. Very rarely it was a woman: the woman might be bracing herself for what my mother was going to say, or if she was lucky not going to say, but to the man she was with. Men were scared of her for themselves—but their women were not scared of her for *them-selves*, it was for the menfolk who were with them.

And you know, that started me trying to think of an instance I could remember of my mother being rough to a woman—and I couldn't, not one. What I could remember, and not only once but two or three times, was of her being *kind* to a woman. Like one time that came into my recollection was when—I told you she did some freelance dressmaking on her own, to bring in a little extra money from time to time, right? Well there was this one time she'd made a dress or something for this woman's daughter, and the woman came and said she was sorry, her husband had just lost his job and he was looking for a new one. So it was going to be maybe a couple of weeks before she could pay the full amount she owed. My mother said that was OK, she didn't mind waiting a little for her money. And you know, I couldn't understand that—because it was only maybe a week before, some poor guy'd come around and told my mother he hadn't the money to pay for something his wife had had made. But you know what she said to him? She said "OK, you bring it straight back then, and you can have it when you can pay for it."

There were other instances too, when she showed some kindness to women. If a woman's husband'd died, she'd give her sympathy, or if he'd been thrown out of work. But if it was the man himself, she couldn't spare a word: either she'd stay ice-cold in silence, or say something unkind about it.

Now what would a psychologist make of that? That she'd been brutally treated by a man herself when she was a child, do you think? We'll never know, will we, except there must have been something in her psyche, mustn't there, to start it all off?

I'll tell you something else about her too. It's been running through my mind a lot lately while I've been working finishing this latest book I'm doing, *Coming of Age,* these interviews with people who're over seventy. I forget who it was now, but a couple of months back I was talking to someone about it and saying what it was about—it wasn't André, so who the hell was it? I forget, I can't remember, anyway it doesn't matter—and they said "*Coming of Age?* That's a lousy title, and a misleading one too. Why don't you call it *Mellowing?*"

I said "*Mellowing?*" Mellowing? That's for wine—but it sure isn't for people. Not everyone in the book is mellow, some of them are pretty goddam furious they're not as young as they used to be, they're doing what Dylan Thomas told his father to do, rage against the dying of the light. So Mellowing's no good . . . heh, why am I on this subject? Oh yeah, I know, my mother. Did she "mellow" as she got older? No sure as hell she did not, she got worse. Like the social worker I told you about, telling Ida she was a monster. Oh boy, there was no mellowing there into a ripe old age, that's for sure.

You wonder what controls these things, don't you? How is it one person grows up to be a cabbage, another one becomes a monster, someone else has all their faculties unimpaired, Bruno Walter and Toscanini conducting Mahler and Beethoven symphonies when they're well in their eighties and they can do it without a score. And Bertrand Russell—he lived to be nearly a hundred!

Now there was a guy. I interviewed him when I went to see him at his home in Penrhyndeudraeth, which I hope is something like the way you pronounce it, and apologize to your Welsh wife for me if it isn't. I went there at the time of the Cuban missile crisis. I don't mind telling you like most other people in the rest of the world, each day for a couple of weeks when I woke up in the morning I wondered if that one was going to be the last one there was.

But Russell! It wasn't just he was ninety so he didn't care that much whether the world blew itself up or not. He *did* care, he cared a lot—particularly for the young people: they were the ones weren't going to have any lives if us and the Russians didn't stop acting like schoolkids in a playground trying to out-dare each other. He cared—but he saw the situation in the round. We sat in armchairs in front of the coal fire in his sitting room full of books and pictures, a lovely view of the sky and the mountains out the window outside—and he spoke in his quiet gentle voice. Just to me, a twangy Chicago-accented American street guy, and he calmed the situation down, gave me a perspective on it, and threw out at me some ideas he had. The way he did it, that was something too: when he talked you realized his long life'd made him give a lot of thought about what he was saying—and when he was saying it, you felt it wasn't he wanted it broadcast from the rooftops, he was trying to share his ideas with you.

I've had some big experiences in my lifetime, but that one I shall always think of as one of the most memorable. Oh and I'll tell you another one that was a good one too, and that was in your country, England, as well. It was meeting your great educator A. S. Neill. You ever heard of him, he had an experimental school named Summerhill, in a town called Leiston or Lyeston in Suffolk County. I went to see him there. What he was doing wasn't just out of the mainstream of education, it was out of the mainstream of the mainstream, you know what I mean? The kids more or less ran the place entirely themselves. There was a school meeting every Saturday night, pupils and staff, and everyone had an equal say. They decided what the timetable of lessons should be, what subjects they should have lessons in, everything—and if you didn't like them, or didn't feel like going to them that day, you didn't go.

Everyone thought he was crazy, naturally. He took the idea of self-government for a school further than anyone else has ever tried to take it, before or since. He stirred up a few hornets' nests in the academic world, specially where lack of control and discipline was concerned, because it included no supervision even over sexual behavior between pupils. So you can imagine. They told me he'd done a couple of books, I think one had an oddball title, *A Dominie's Log* or something like that. "Dominie" is the word the Scots use for "schoolmaster," I think. And the other was called *Neill! Neill! Orange Peel!*, which is what the kids in his school called him, so I read them both and then I went to visit with him.

The great thing about the guy, the way I saw it, was that he shook the education establishment up, you know? He kind of challenged all the accepted ideas about how things should be between teachers and pupils. He made people ask themselves whether what they were doing was right or not, if they were working from correct assumptions. If in the end they decided they were, and his ideas were crazy, leastways he'd made them think and not go on every day in the same old way without giving any thought to it.

Yeah, good question. How the hell did I hear about him in the first place? How was it, was it something I read in a newspaper or what? Let me think about it a minute. Got it, I know how it was, it was Hugh MacDiarmid, the Scottish poet. It was when we were talking after I'd interviewed *him*. He was the one told me about A. S. Neill and said he was someone I should talk to. Yeah, MacDiarmid, that's who it was. He was the poet leading the Scots literary renaissance, or trying to bring it about, that's more the truth of it. He was researching into the old Scottish dialect called "Lallans" if I've got the name right, hoping to rescue it from obscurity. One person putting you on to another. That happens a lot. "Accretion of accidents" again, right?

And now there was an example of something lost through my technical ineptitude with the tape recorder, my interview with MacDiarmid. Would you believe, I never got a word of it, not one word? I pressed the wrong switch on the machine so it looked to me like it was recording. But it wasn't. I always hate machines of any kind. I'm suspicious they're going to let you down—and they do. Boy, there was so much I missed on that English trip through not being able to work the goddam machine properly. I interviewed Michael Redgrave in his dressing room at the theater, I think it was The Haymarket or some place—then when I came to play it back to myself to listen to when I'm back here at home, all I have is that soft, hiss hissing of unrecorded tape.

Peter Hall, he was another one I missed. And Peter Brook, he was another one too. And there's no going back and doing it again. I nearly missed out on Bertrand Russell as well, I was only just in time on that one. "Excuse me, Lord Russell, hold on one moment please while I press the right button—yeah, that's OK now, go ahead, the world can explode too if it wants to, the sound's switched on." I had to say that—well, nearly all of it. Have I made some goofs in my time? Are you serious?

I guess the only thing consoles me a bit is it's other people who think *they* know what *they're* doing, once in a while they louse up too. The classic for me, one I *wasn't* responsible for, was when I interviewed Jacques Tati, the great French film comic. And *that* was in the studio, because they didn't trust me on the loose on my own with a tape recorder. So how about that?

He comes in one morning and we have this great conversation and Jacques Tati's in tremendous form about one of his favorite themes, which is how the human spirit is being submerged by technology. But he hopes and believes there's always room for the human touch, he's sure that will triumph in the end. Chaplin in *Modern Times,* all that sort of thing. And Tati's great, he's really great. We do this whole long interview, then we do the windup, and then we finish. And I'm sitting there chatting with him, feeling pretty good about the way it's gone.

Then the door behind him opens and the young engineer from the recording control-room comes in. And he stands there signaling to me, and he's trembling and his face is white. So I went around to him and I said "What is it, what's the matter?" And he says, hoping we won't be heard, "I don't know how to tell you this but I didn't get it. I overlooked pressing the final 'record' button, there's nothing on the tape. Have we got time to do it again?"

Well Tati can hear this whispering, and he turns around and looks, and he can see this young guy standing there with his face so white. And me too then I guess, looking the same. So he doesn't need to ask a question, he only has to look. And he looks for a moment, and then he says "There is nothing on the tape?" And I can't speak, but I nod my head slowly several times like this "Yes that's right, there's nothing on the tape." The engineer, he can't speak either, so he *shakes* his head slowly like this, "No, there's nothing on the tape." And there's a pause for a moment—and then you know what? Tati bursts out in a great roar of laughter! "There you are!" he says. "It is just like I have been saying, is it not? All this wonderful modern machinery you have for a recording, and it does not work!"

He couldn't stay on with us that day, he couldn't do the interview again: and if he had you know, I don't think it'd have been good, the spontaneity wouldn't have been there. But he was very gracious about it, he said why didn't we come around to his hotel the next day at three in the afternoon, bring all our equipment we needed, and we'd record another interview. They didn't trust me to go on my own, so they sent an engineer with me to operate the gear, so I had that worry off my mind. We did it again, and this time we got it.

But it was different from the first one, completely. In its way, I think it was just as good, or even better. Something else happened, which he used as a starting-off point for something different he wanted to say. As it happened the day of our visit was his birthday. The hotel knew it, I guess they keep a diary of all things like that to do with their famous guests. So we'd been there maybe ten minutes or so and were setting up our gear, when there was a knock at the door, and in sweeps the hotel manager. The maître d' of the restaurant was with him, and a few other of the people who work there—plus some press photographers. And they're carrying a birthday cake as big as this they've made for him, which they present to him, compliments of the hotel. We all had to have our picture taken with it for the newspapers, and then they all made to go out again. Naturally nothing would satisfy Tati except that everybody should have a piece, so plates and a knife were sent for, he cuts the cake, and everybody munches down a slice.

When that little ceremony's out of the way and the hotel people are out of the way too, and we can start getting on with our interview, just before we begin Tati says to me "So—what did you think of the cake?" I hadn't been too impressed with it. "It was OK" I said. "It was good." He could see that I was being polite, and he hadn't taken too great a liking to it himself either. So he said "Well" he said, "let us be frank, it was terrible, yes? But you see what it is—it is a metaphor we can use in our conversation, how often these days we have a great panoply and ceremony about something that of itself, if we are honest, is not any good." So that was our theme, which we quickly got onto, not directly using the cake or the hotel of course, but having an interview which came out fine.

You were going to say something earlier? England? Oh England, yeah, how come I was seeing so many people in England that time? Well, I've been there a lot, mostly to be interviewed or do some work. The way I work it usually is I wait until somebody asks me there for some specific thing, and if I want to do it, when we've got the dates fixed, I let friends know in advance I'm coming, say like Eleanor, and I ask other people I know if they can fix up for me to meet people I'd like to meet.

It might have nothing to do with the original reason for me going there in the first place. I take the opportunity, that's how I work it. And then some person I meet'll say "Heh, while you're here you ought to go and see so and so"—like MacDiarmid putting me on to A. S. Neill. Sometimes I get around and meet so many people, I can't hardly remember how I came to be there in the first place. "What brought you to England?" they say, and I have to say "Let me think."

But there was one time I remember, the original reason for coming, now that was really something special. One of your I think you call them "commercial" TV stations, they asked me over because after *Working* and *Hard Times* had come out in England, they had the idea of putting out a big thirteen-part series about a similar time in Britain to our Depression years. They were going to concentrate on the 1920s and early thirties, times of big unemployment and people's memories of how it was. They thought it'd give it a kind of original slant if an American narrated it and interviewed the people involved, so they asked me to come over and do it.

It was all to be filmed in a two-to-three-week period, and it was a nice little assignment. They found the locations and a whole lot of people for me to talk to—residents of an old-people's home, a retired London cop, a guy who'd been a political activist, someone who'd been on the hunger march from Jarrow to London, a couple of music hall people, and some others—and they were going to mix these interviews in with old film. I didn't see it when it went out, but I heard it turned into a pretty good show.

I'll tell you though about the thing I remember best about doing it. We all went out to a very smart big house in the countryside, me and the camera crew and the rest, to interview a lady whose name escapes me at the moment. Well it doesn't escape me, I know it very well, but I'm not going to say it. She's quite famous, she's not exactly a member of your Royal Family but she almost is. She behaves as if she is too. She's elderly, you could even say good and old, she dresses in frills and furs and flounces, and her face and skin are covered in makeup from here to here. Oh yes, and I believe she writes a bit too, though I can't say I've read any of her books.

So there we are and we arrive at her house, and we're told her Lady-ship's expecting us and we're to go on upstairs—up a great big marble staircase to her bedroom. And there she is, waiting to receive us—in her bedroom—in bed! She's reclining graciously in a big high-collared ruf-fled and quilted and beribboned negligee, scented and powdered and ringed and bejeweled, and if she wasn't fluttering a fan around as well she sure gave the impression she was! And it's "Oh my darlings, come in come in, how wonderful to see you, isn't this wonderful, how kind of you to want to talk to me! Oh I do hope I'm not going to disappoint you, now you just put your lights wherever you want to to get the best effect. Now you will forgive me if I'm nervous won't you?"

Well, the guys in the crew can hardly believe it, you know. And what with the perfume floating around them and everything, they're dizzy with it all. But let me tell you, believe me, what they saw that made them giddy and cross-eyed, that was nothing to what they felt when they heard after she started to talk.

It didn't take her long when I asked her for her recollections about poverty and unemployment in the twenties to start in about the 1926 General Strike. She was in London at that time and she was a girl of twenty-five. And as she told it, tears started to run down her cheeks, real tears. She said "Seeing all those people standing at street corners, no work for them, no money to buy food with, oh it was terrible, it broke your heart, it was so sad." Then she said "Wherever you went in London on the buses you know, you saw it everywhere, north of the river, south of the river, in the West End and the East End, it was all exactly the same." I said "But how come you could see them in so many places from the buses, weren't the buses on strike too?" "Oh yes" she said, "only like all the other young people, you know, me and my friends, we all volunteered to drive the buses to keep them running. Everyone needed them to get around, you see, you couldn't just let London come to a standstill, could you?" And all the guys with me you know, the camera crew and the soundmen and the lighting guys, they're all trades unionists, aren't they? They couldn't work in those jobs if they didn't belong to the different technicians' unions: I didn't have to look round, I could hear the sound of the hair bristling up on the backs of their necks. And there she is, still crying and sniffing into her handkerchief and saying "Oh all those poor people, seeing them looking so without hope like that, it was so sad, so sad."

I wound it up as quick as I could, I'll tell you. And you know, she wasn't aware of the atmosphere, not even that much. In a couple of minutes the tears were gone, she was looking in her hand mirror to see whether it had damaged her makeup, and back playing the gracious hostess with "Thank you so much for coming to see me" and all the rest of it. And then finally, you know what she did? She pulled her bell-cord for her maid, and she said to us "Now before you go, I want to give you all a little souvenir of your visit"—and in comes her maid with a tray already prepared with a little pot of honey for each of us on it, and hands them around. "Now I want you to have these" says the great lady, "because you know what honey does for you, don't you? It increases your sexual potency!"

Boy, you've heard the expression "dumbstruck"? Well, every one of us, every single one, were struck dumb. We filed out of there without a word, with her "Good-bye. Good-byyyee!" from the bedroom getting fainter and fainter in the background as we went down the stairs. Whether the television company ever included that interview in the series I wouldn't know. I shouldn't think they did, what with my incredulous questions, and I guess the film shaking more and more while the cameraman was shooting.

Memories of England, eh . . . ? Oh boy!

6

Voices in the Air

Pete Seeger	Zero Mostel
Dorothy Parker	Lord Bertrand Russell
Simone de Beauvoir	Andrés Segovia
James Baldwin	Kenneth Tynan
Tennessee Williams	Dame Margot Fonteyn
Isaac Bashevis Singer	Mahalia Jackson

These are brief extracts from tape-recorded interviews in a four-cassette anthology entitled Four Decades with Studs Terkel, produced by Tom Voegeli and published by HighBridge Company, St. Paul, Minnesota.

Pete Seeger

Studs: We'll start with one of the very many conversations I've had with Pete Seeger, whom I might call the tuning fork of American folk song. Whenever you see a young singer with his banjo held high and his Adam's apple bobbing, you know that, like Kilroy, Pete Seeger was there. And here he is, talking of what he described as the family of folk song.

Seeger: I've always thought of Casey Jones as being just one member of a very large family of railroad-worker songs. You know the song about Jay Gould's daughter?

(Sings and plays)

> "Charlie Snyder was a good engineer
> Told his fireman not to fear.
> Put on your water boys
> Shovel out the coal
> And see the driver's roll
> The driver's roll
> See the driver's roll
> Stick your head out the window
> And see the driver's roll."

That same verse comes up in Casey Jones.

Studs: Who was Charlie Snyder?

Seeger: Well just some other man got killed in some other railroad
           accident, I guess. What happens when someone writes a song is
           he makes it up in the first place out of fragments of other
           songs. He swipes a tune, he swipes a verse, he puts it together,
           and if it's a good song it'll become popular and it'll spread
           around. Then somebody else hears it maybe a hundred years
           later, an event happens which reminds him of it, and he
           changes around the old song to fit the new event.

Studs: Wasn't it Ollie Saunders who wrote the Casey Jones song? And
           he'd heard the Charlie Snyder song?

Seeger: Oh I'm sure, because he couldn't have made the song up just
           out of nothing. That's why they're all like cousins in a family—
           first cousins, second cousins, third cousins, until they've got so
           far off you can hardly recognize they have a relationship.

Studs: I heard you sing one some time ago, "John Dooley" was it,
           "Tom Dooley," something like that?

Seeger: "Tom Dooley." That was a nice song. I've been told it was a
           post–Civil War song. Tom Dooley was a soldier, and he came
           home and found his girl had been unfaithful to him.

Studs: How does it go?

Seeger: Maybe the listeners'll sing along, it's such a nice song.
           (Sings and plays)

> "Hang down your head, Tom Dooley
> Hang down your head and cry
> Hang down your head, Tom Dooley
> Poor boy you're bound to die."

And then it goes on

> "I met her on the mountain
> And there I took her life
> I met her on the mountain
> And stabbed her with my knife."

Then the chorus again.

"Hang down your head, Tom Dooley
'Fetch me down my banjo
I'll pick it on my knee
This time tomorrow
I'll hang from a white oak tree.'
Hang down your head, Tom Dooley . . ."

I can't remember all the verses.

Studs: That's fine Pete, that's great.

Dorothy Parker

Studs: *And this was Dorothy Parker, celebrated wit and critic, famed for her mordant humor and the sharpness of her tongue.*

Studs: Across me at the table is a writer of short stories, poetry, plays, drama criticism and often maker of most piercing remarks—Dorothy Parker. But she's also a person of great compassion, and she actually likes far more people than she dislikes. Is that a fair appraisal, Mrs. Parker?

Parker: It's much too fair. I thought you were talking about somebody else.

Studs: I was thinking about your writings and want to ask you a rather sad question to open our conversation with—which is, what's happened to American humor?

Parker: I think there's only ever been one real humorist in America, and that's S. J. Perelman who wrote all the Marx brothers' film scripts. I think there aren't any being born any more. Or perhaps we don't want humor any more, there's no supply because there's no demand. As far as satire's concerned, I feel the English are much better at it too than we are, but I don't know why. We don't have the ability to laugh at ourselves, and that's a very grave fault. Perhaps it's due to insecurity. Or it might be apathy, I really don't know. We used to have poets who were supposed to belong to something called "the Beat Generation," and they made a lot of noise but it was all about nothing. Now they're as out of date as mah-jongg.

Simone de Beauvoir

He interviewed Simone de Beauvoir in her apartment in Paris not long after her book The Second Sex *had brought her considerable fame both in Europe and in the United States. She and her companion Jean-Paul Sartre were also well known as the leading existentialists of the time.*

Studs: How did you become a writer?

de Beauvoir: Well in my family we were rather poor, and my mother was a very pious woman but my father didn't believe in God, so it made for a discrepancy. But he very much respected my mother's belief and the way she educated my sister and myself, and they both encouraged us to do a lot of reading about God and sin and war and such things, and decide for ourselves what we wanted to believe in and to do with our lives. By the time I had come to be fifteen I had made up my mind to be a student and a writer, and I became determined. André Gide's books had a great influence on me when I was twenty, when he wrote about being oneself and being free, which was something I wanted very much.

Studs: How did being a woman affect that?

de Beauvoir: Well in a good way I think, because I had an intellectually very steady life and knew I could do as I wanted. I never resented being a woman at all, I look upon myself as a human being among other human beings and it was to stress that that I wrote *The Second Sex*. But it did not come from personal problems because being a woman was not a personal problem to me.

James Baldwin

James Baldwin was a young novelist who had written The Fire Next Time *and* Notes of a Native Son. *He was revisiting America, where he was born, although he had been living in Switzerland when he started writing.*

Baldwin: That winter there in Switzerland when I was working on my first novel, I thought I'd never be able to finish it because I was so ashamed of what I was—of my father, of blues music, of liking watermelon—of all the stereotypical things that all the white people around me inflicted on me because I was black. I realized that I hadn't even always talked the way I did, I'd forced myself into doing it, and I wasn't speaking with what were really my natural cadences. I'd told myself lies. So I played Bessie Smith records every day to learn how a genuine Negro should sound. And I really had to dig down into myself and learn who I was, and then force the white world to deal with me as I was, and not with its own image of me.

Studs: You have something coming out, I believe, don't you, called *Nobody Knows My Name?*

Baldwin: That's right. For years nobody knew me as James Baldwin, it was usually George Baldwin, or even in the bad old days just sometimes "boy." When people do that now, I don't answer.

Studs: You're invisible to them.

Baldwin: I'm invisible to them, right. Which is terrible, because half the white people and the black people in the South here are physically related to each other somewhere in the past generations. They all have to learn to live together. They have to. You have to educate young people to think, and as it is now this is something they just cannot think about.

Studs: We don't even know our own names?

Baldwin: Precisely. That's precisely the point.

Tennessee Williams

One of the less successful interviews, due to the malfunctioning of the tape recorder—or Studs's inability to get it functioning properly—was with the play-wright Tennessee Williams, whom he interviewed in his hotel suite when he visited Chicago.

Studs: Mr. Williams, the theater critic Kenneth Tynan once wrote of your love for what he called "incomplete people." Would you go along with that?

Williams: Oh yes. I've always regarded myself as an incomplete person and consequently I've always been interested in my own kind of people. People who come close to cracking, that's my life and those are my people and I write about the people I know. I'm sure it must limit me as an artist but I couldn't write believable characters if I moved outside that world. But that doesn't mean I'm all together a crackpot because I'm not.

Studs: Are these basically sensitive people in a brutal framework?

Williams: I think of course they are. Give a person an acute sensibility and you're bound to find a person who is under a good deal of torment.

Studs: Tell me about the character of Blanche du Bois for instance.

Williams: Well, she said "I don't tell truth, I tell what ought to be truth." She had the courage to admit she occasionally embel-lished upon the real facts, and when her back was to the wall she had courage and truth and eloquence, I thought.

Studs: Something you wrote that's very often quoted is "We are all in solitary confinement in our own skins." Is that—

Williams: Well it's "solitary confinement inside our own skins."

Studs: Is that from *Orpheus*?

Williams: Yeah. The drama in my plays is nearly always people trying to reach each other: they're confined inside their own skins but they must try to get out and find a truly satisfying contact. I don't just mean a physical contact, I mean a deeper contact than that where they can—

(The tape goes blank.)

Isaac Bashevis Singer

Many people consider the Polish-born American Isaac Bashevis Singer to be the greatest Yiddish writer there has ever been. He was awarded the Nobel Prize for literature in 1978.

Studs: Mr. Singer, you're always concerned, aren't you, with dreams and fantasy and demons, and the narrow line between them and reality?

Singer: Well the truth is that in life itself it's so short a way between fantasy and reality that I would say there's almost no difference between them. So I would say in many cases, it's likely it should be in literature because literature is not only an account of what a man does but also of how he feels—what he thinks and what is in his mind, and in the mind fantasy is certainly almost everything. Many of my stories are written so that they are ambiguous. In other words if you are a rationalist you can find an explanation, and if you are a believer you can find another explanation.

Studs: You leave it open even though you write definitely?

Singer: Yes. You can reason but still have a choice. I consider myself a kind of mystic.

Studs: Would you expand on that?

Singer: What I mean is what we know about life and ourselves is not everything. There are hidden powers which we may never know. For example telepathy is such a power. We all have it although we don't know why, or how it works. The same thing is true about dreams which come true. I would say that there is some mystic in every human being, even in those who deny it. I believe that we have lived many times already. There's no evidence for it, but this is my personal feeling, that we have been here before, are here now, and may be here again and again. You don't find it in the Bible but you find it in the Talmud, this belief in transfiguration, that we come here again and again.

Studs: You think we've been here before?

Singer: I'm not sure we had an interview on the radio before, because there was no radio before I was born.

Studs: What do you think is missing in literature today?

Singer: I think mainly that a writer is not sure of himself and his mission, as they were for example in the nineteenth century. Writers like Tolstoy and Dostoyevsky believed literature could do a lot for human beings, to help them, but modern writers are almost resigned that they cannot.

Studs: To use the currently fashionable word, are they alienated?

Singer: Many of them. But they should not be, because they are a part of humanity. And they should write with passion, because without passion you cannot have *com*passion either. I had not thought of that connection between those two words until now, it is good how you get people to say these things.

Zero Mostel

The interview with the irrepressible film and stage comedian Zero Mostel was of a somewhat different kind.

Studs: Today as my guest this morning I have with me one of the greatest clowns of our day, Zero Mostel. Zero—may I call you "Zero"—?

Mostel: Call it to me to my face.

Studs: Zero—

Mostel: Thank you.

Studs: Zero, one of the first questions I'd like to ask you is a generalized one.

Mostel: You want a generalized answer?

Studs: No I want a specific one.

Mostel: You want a specific answer to a generalized question? You're crazy. OK go ahead.

Studs: What are your feelings about being a clown?

Mostel: Well it's interesting that in French the word for "actor" is comedian, and they think always of him in that sense, as someone who heightens the drama and makes it larger than life. And I think that's what theater should be in whatever form it is, comedy or anything else. When you see W. C. Fields for example, you see great theater, in all that dignity he carries against the terrible things in life, and it was a marvellous attitude he conveyed, that despite everything he was a good human being. He makes us see such things.

Studs: You too of course are a good actor and a good comic—

Mostel: And a good son.

Studs: And a good son.

Mostel: And a good father.

Studs: And a good father.

Mostel: And a good mother.

Studs: *(Laughing)* Yes.

Mostel: Where was I?

Studs: You were talking about Fields making us see things.

Mostel: Yes, as all artists do. Painters show us things, action painters like Jackson Pollock, or Rembrandt, or Picasso—and then you get the guy who comes walking out of an exhibition of somebody like that and he says "I don't dig it."

Studs: "I don't know anything about art—"

Mostel: "—but I know what I like." Right. It reminds me of the joke about the editor of the newspaper who advertised he wanted an interpreter, and this guy comes in and says "I've come applying to the job of interpreter you're advertising." So the editor says to him, he says "Do you speak English?" and the guy says "What for? Why should I speak English, I'm Jewish." So the editor says "Do you speak German?" "No" the guy says, "I'm Jewish, why should I speak German?" "Italian?" "Oh" he says, "a beautiful language but I can't speak it, no." "French?" "Also very beautiful. Not as beautiful as Italian, though no, I don't speak French either." "Look" says the editor, "what did you come here for?" The guy says "I came to tell you not to depend on me."

Lord Bertrand Russell

He spoke with the ninety-year-old mathematician and philosopher Bertrand Russell at his home in Penrhyndeudrath, North Wales, in 1962 during the time of the Cuban missile crisis.

Studs: Lord Russell, sitting here in this delightful room on a lovely sunny Tuesday morning, the scene is so peaceful and yet the world outside is so rife with tension, what you yourself have called "the insane drive of America and Russia towards mutual destruction"—Let me ask you a leading question—which side are you on?

Russell: I'm not on either side, it is folly and I want the contest to die down, just as after a great storm the waves of the sea get less.

Studs: I believe you said in one of your lectures recently "The two large powers, East and West, the Soviet Union and the United States, have so much in common that nine-tenths of their interests are identical and it's only in the matter of their ideology that they differ."

Russell: I did, and I don't think ideology plays an important part whatever in the differences between them. It's just a question of which is to have power.

Studs: But individuals all over the world feel they can't do anything about it.

Russell: That is a mistake. They can. An individual can do a very great deal simply by expressing an opinion. The powerlessness of the individual is a pretense, an alibi for doing nothing, a form of cowardice almost. There are three requisites for a stable world—one is that one government should have a monopoly of all the weapons in the world so that nobody could fight against it, the second is that people should cease to hold the view that was held by the Inquisition and is still held by the majority of mankind, that a person who disagrees should be exterminated. And thirdly there should be a raising of the level of the standard of living in the underdeveloped countries so that their people are as well-off as the people of the United States. In that way the poor would not envy the rich, and the rich need not fear the poor.

Studs: Would you say most young people of today are with you on that?

Russell: I would hope so, because you see most young people want to live. It does not matter much to me because I am old whether I die in a nuclear war or not, because I should probably die around that time anyway. But young people don't feel like that: they have life ahead of them, and they want to be allowed to live it. They don't want someone to say "No, you have to be wiped out just to please us and so we can win the next election."

Andrés Segovia

When he spoke with Andrés Segovia, the classical guitarist, Studs asked him how it had come about that he had chosen to play the guitar rather than the violin or the piano.

Segovia: Because first, I was born with the vocation for music, and the musicians who play in the little village where I was growing, who played the piano, the violin, the cello, they were very mediocre. And I rejected the sound of the piano and the violin and the cello because they were mediocre, they were terrible. A friend of mine used to say the piano was like a rectangular monster of which you touched her teeth.

Studs: So you taught yourself to play the guitar?

Segovia: Well I heard the guitar playing by the people, and although they play with very rough hands, the sound, very melancholy, attracted me. So I tried to musicalize the guitar, because I hear always around me the flamenco guitar and I didn't like it. The flamenco is very beautiful, but the way they play it—no. I saw in the instrument the delicacy that it had: it had a graceful feminine quality, on account of the curves of the guitar.

Kenneth Tynan

Kenneth Tynan of The Observer *was interviewed in London. He had been a visiting theatre critic for two years for* The New York Times.

Studs: You caused quite a stir with your reviews in America. What are your feelings in retrospect about the state of the American theatre's health?

Tynan: Well what used to madden me about the American theatre was I had never seen so much talent put to so much ill-use. I don't think you can tie the amount of energy, talent and exuberance in the American theatre permanently to the tyranny of the box office because eventually somebody is going to get up and say as Matthew Arnold did, "The Theatre is irresistible! Organize the theatre!" He said it in an article advocating the cause of a subsidized National Theatre with a permanent theatre company, and I think that's what's missing in the American theatre. Coming into town with a play that's had an exhausting out-of-town tour with seventy-five rewrites and everyone changing lines because they might not appeal to Broadway producers—well this doesn't seem to me the way to handle talent. It seemed to me cruel, and the more I saw playwrights and actors put through this mincer on Broadway, the more I felt legitimate theatre there was dwindling and was suffering a bad case of commercial shell shock. The sort of plays that are now put on Broadway tend to be those that people think will be surefire successes—that's to say they're mostly large-scale musicals. When you do get the odd adult play, like *Who's Afraid of Virginia Woolf?* for instance, it's an oasis. As a drama critic on Broadway I felt I was becoming more of an obituarist than anything else. Four out of five plays I reviewed would be closed before my notice appeared. And one hates to make a living always writing about something in the past tense.

Studs: Is there more chance for experimental drama in Europe?

Tynan: Yes for purely economic reasons. It costs a quarter of what it costs to put on a play here than in the States, and so you can keep the privilege to flop, the right to fail, which I think in the

States is lacking. If Shakespeare had had to operate under those kind of conditions he'd probably have turned out only about a third of what he did. I think that's what kept Arthur Miller off Broadway so long.

Dame Margot Fonteyn

He spoke with prima ballerina Margot Fonteyn shortly after her book, based on her BBC Television series The Magic of the Dance, *appeared.*

Studs: Your book doesn't concern yourself directly. When did you know that you wanted to be a dancer?

Fonteyn: I don't know when I first knew, because I was always a dancer from before I can remember.

Studs: Really? From way back in the beginning?

Fonteyn: Well my mother took me to dancing classes when I was three or three and a half, I can't remember exactly when it was. But it's always seemed the most natural thing in the world for me to have been a dancer. And when I was fourteen I went to Sadler's Wells and became a professional. And then every summer I used to go to Paris and studied with some of the great ballerinas of the past, who were then in their sixties and seventies, and really got the great traditions from them first hand, it was marvellous.

Studs: Did Ninette de Valois come to Sadler's Wells?

Fonteyn: Well Ninette de Valois was at the turn of the century and then we'd never thought of England and ballet very much. In the nineteenth century all the great stars and choreographers went to places where there were dance patrons like the Paris Opera, and St. Petersburg and Moscow and Copenhagen, but we never had that in England.

Studs: Some of the old-time dancers there are pictures of in your book look really great. The illustrations are marvelous. Martha Graham—

Fonteyn: A superb picture of Martha Graham isn't it? Something that always makes me laugh is that picture of people doing the waltz there. It seems to us a pretty harmless dance doesn't it? But when it first became popular at the beginning of the nineteenth century, many people thought it horribly shocking and indecent—and there's a quotation there from the London *Times* where it's described as "a lascivious intertwining of the limbs"! But then finally Herself—everybody called her "Herself"—Queen Victoria—she danced the waltz with Prince Albert, and that made it respectable. And another funny thing was that all the people who'd been writing and talking against the waltz and saying how shocking it was, they all said the same thing that people still say nowadays when they object to something. They said "We feel it our duty to warn fathers against letting their daughters do this"!

Studs: And you have pictures of Isadora Duncan and write about her too, don't you?

Fonteyn: Yes. She's very often credited with being the mother of modern dance, but I can't see that. She was only modern in the sense that she didn't do ballet dancing. She thought it was boring and stilted, and she was a very emotional woman and very musical, and so she always danced to Beethoven and Brahms and Chopin, which ballet dancers hadn't thought of doing, and so she created a great sensation. She was trying to liberate the body because when she watched people standing and walking on their toes it was ungraceful and unnatural and she loathed it.

Studs: Well we have to stop there. Thank you very much indeed, Margot Fonteyn. Is there any last thing you'd like to say?

Fonteyn: Only thank you—and I'm glad I'm a dancer. And I think you're a dancer too.

Studs: Well maybe at heart perhaps.

Fonteyn: Yes yes, at heart you are.

Mahalia Jackson

He's always said that if anybody could have "saved" him and reconverted him to religious belief, it would have been the black gospel singer, Mahalia Jackson. His last recorded radio conversation with her before she died begins with her singing a song called "You Got to Keep Moving and You Got to Have Heart."

Studs: Mahalia, you and I have known each other what, now, about seventeen years?

Mahalia: That's right.

Studs: And I'm thinking about you and that song, and I want to ask you what does it mean for you today?

Mahalia: Well Studs, it means you got to keep moving and you got to have heart and you got to keep suffering. Because in this world there is so many people trying to move, they got to just keep pushing away. There is so many people ready to move, to come out of poverty and to come out of oppression, and that's the meaning of it. You're trying to tell the world you've got to have a heart and a soul and a real feeling of love in your heart when you're trying to move on and success is to love each other.

Studs: It's pretty difficult though isn't it?

Mahalia: No. It's sad.

Studs: It's difficult because it's rough to turn the other cheek though isn't it?

Mahalia: Well that's the Lord's teaching isn't it, and I've gone along with it pretty much to follow His leadership. It's pretty hard for someone to keep knocking you down, and He keeps saying "Stick to it." I know He's right. But I can get a little angry there you know, especially when they put the little children into jail. The only thing we're interested in is equal rights, and we can make a living to survive, you understand? And to have an education, like the grace of God has brought me. I was an unlearned woman, and down South there was nothing for me to do but push the white people's buggies and their babies' buggies, and clean their babies and clean their houses. Just since I been up North a little bit of opportunities open, but a thing that puzzles me is that since I've been on stage and television white people hug me and love me and tell me I'm wonderful and I'm great—but when I'm walking down the street like an ordinary citizen they don't recognize me. And when I go in a department store I can't get a sandwich, I can't get a bottle of pop, and outside I can't get a cab—but I'm just the same Mahalia Jackson that they got to saying how wonderful I was. What I don't understand is what makes people act like that. I want to see my people respected you know, it's a most distasteful thing to hear a white man call my husband or my brother "boy." That's disrespect, that's the height of ignorance for people to treat other people like that. I'm so hurt about it it keeps me praying to the Lord not to let hate get into my heart. It'd make you think you'd go down the drain with despair, and I don't believe in nothing like that getting so deep in my soul, so I speak out about it so I can be free. Because if it stays inside I'll be a hateful woman, and I don't want to hate, I want to love. The Reverend Dr. Martin Luther King, he said, "Walk together, children, don't get weary," and he said "The promised land is right here in America." I was born here, and I expect to die right here. And if they kill me, then I'll be buried in the land of the free. And we'll all walk together right here, and sing together, and shout together, and also fight together.

Studs: And you're on your way.

Mahalia: I'm on my way.

(She sings the song "Moving on Together, High and Low")

7

English Friends

Eleanor Bron, Actress

Cedric Price, Architect

Joan Littlewood, Theatre Director

Lady Moni Forman

Mike Dibb, Television Producer

Eleanor Bron, Actress

Smiling with pleasure at recollections, she sat talking quietly and swinging herself gently to and fro on a brightly floral-patterned sofa-hammock in the sitting room of her flat in London.

—I first met Studs, well not exactly met, I suppose a more correct word would be encountered him—in Chicago, ages ago, it must be more than thirty years ago now. John Bird and I and other members of a show called *The Establishment,* which was a satirical revue we were in in London, took it to America to Chicago and New York and he—Studs—interviewed us all—the whole cast—on his radio chat show. Two things amazed me about him; one was how much he knew about the English political background and the people in it who we were, well, mocking is I suppose the right word, and what a knowledgeable basis that gave him to draw on for his questioning—I'm sure no Englishman would know anything like that amount about the ins and outs of the contemporary American scene. And the other thing was how clever it was of him to interview the whole group of us all together. I think there were about four or five of us, but he didn't ask us questions in turn one after the other, he got us all talking to each other as well as to him. It was very clever of him, and gave the whole thing a very easy and natural atmosphere which was quite unlike anything I've experienced ever before or since.

After that, whenever I was in America on my own for one reason or another, I always met him in Chicago or New York if I could: and if that wasn't possible I'd call him up on the phone and we'd have long chats together. I'm a great keeper-in-touch with people, or I used to be more than I am now, and so's he: whenever he's in England, which sadly isn't too often these days, he always gets in touch with me and we have a meal together. One of the nicest things I do find about him—I'm sure other people who know him do too—is the length of time there's been between when you see each other doesn't matter in the least: you always start talking straight away from where you left off last time, and it's lovely when you can do that, it's how a real friendship should be.

Over the years I've got to know and be friends with his wife Ida as well, and she's a person I'm very fond of too. In manner she's nothing like the ebullient character Studs is, but she has a very strong personality all her own, and doesn't live at all in his shadow. She's very much a thinker and a person of deep political convictions, and she's very actively involved in causes she believes in. She doesn't compromise and never has: I admire very much her integrity, and the way she's not been content just to be the wife of a famous person and's always been her own woman. She has the same kind of what I can only describe as energy for life as he has, and they complement each other wonderfully.

Studs is very generous in spirit and he displays it often in quite an embarrassing way. He sometimes tells people—I don't know if he's told you yet—that I'm the person who's responsible for him beginning to write books and I'm the one who set him on the path to making his reputation as an oral historian. It's a story that's come back to me several times, that he's said this: and it's a perfect example of Studs's giving far more credit to someone than they're entitled to. There's a slight amount of truth in it, but not as much as all that: he's grossly exaggerating. What happened is that André Schiffrin, his American editor and publisher, was a friend of mine when we were both at Cambridge University. After my first meeting with Studs in Chicago that I told you about, we then went on to perform our revue in New York, and while I was there I looked up André, who by then had a job as an editor at Pantheon Books, and his wife. André'd not long before that published an oral history portrait of a Chinese village by an anthropologist, and all I did when we were talking about it was ask him if he knew Studs's work and tell him how good I thought it was.

André was then—and still is now—very much the sort of publisher who goes out looking for books and persuading people to write them: he doesn't just sit around all day waiting for them to come to him. I think anyway he'd already read one or two things by Studs, odd pieces in magazines and so on, so I don't think he'd not ever heard of him. And that's all there was to it—but dear sweet old Studs is always telling people it's me who deserves all the credit. I'm quite sure he and André would have met anyway before long somehow, and the result would have been the same. And anyway even if I ever did do any slight favor at all for him, he's since repaid me a hundred times, because it was at a party he once gave that I met Cedric.

I've never appeared in one of his books, but in the intervening years, on the odd occasion when I've been in Chicago in a play or something he's asked me on to his radio program. I remember once I read I think it was a Marguerite Duras short story, and another time I read an excerpt from *Madame Bovary*. And he's interviewed me on my own a couple of times.

Usually I don't like doing solo interviews because you always get plied with all the stock questions which you know you're going to be asked—like—"What is it you like about this character?" and you give all your usual stock answers "Well you see I feel she's like me in so many ways" and all that kind of rubbish. But with Studs it's nothing like that ever—and what's always so good is that even knowing that, it doesn't scare you: you look forward to the experience, or at least I always do, and don't dread it in any way.

It's hard to put it into words, but it's almost as if, well, let's say for example you've got a chest of drawers. And you decide which one or which ones you're going to open to show a friend what's inside, and take things out of the drawer to show them. With Studs it's exactly like that: you do all the deciding about which drawer to open, which things to take out and show him—and it's entirely up to you, he never bullies you or tries to trick you into revealing something you don't want to. Then when you hold it up for him to look at, he looks at it with you. He's tremendously interested in it, and as a result you become reinterested in it, and you start to see it in a new light—and it becomes a really enjoyable conversational experience.

I don't know if any of that's of any help to you, I'm not very good at expressing myself I'm afraid.

Cedric Price, Architect

In his offices off Tottenham Court Road in central London, one small room is decorated and furnished entirely in white, with sketches and unframed photographs of modern buildings on the walls. It's kept for chatting in with clients and colleagues, or merely for just sitting quietly and thinking in. A tall deep-voiced man with dark hair, he clasped his hands behind his head and sat looking out of the window at the barely audible traffic below.

—Studs? Oh yes, it's always a pleasure to meet someone who knows him. I met him myself through Joan Littlewood: I'd been working with her on an idea she and I'd had for a kind of amusement garden somewhere on the banks of the Thames, and I happened to mention to her that in a few weeks' time I was going to the United States to lecture at a couple of universities there. She said while I was there, if by any chance I happened to be passing through Chicago or be anywhere near it, please would I telephone a friend of hers called Studs Terkel and say hello to him from her.

I forget exactly which particular universities they were now, but about seven o'clock one morning I found myself in Chicago's O'Hare Airport waiting to change planes and catch one for Detroit. I had about an hour in hand before I was due to fly out again, so I took Joan at her word and rang Studs at his home and gave him her message. Even though we'd never met, his response was typical. He asked where I was, and when I told him he said "Have you had any breakfast yet?" I said no I hadn't so he said "Well why don't you take a cab and come over and have some with my wife and me and then take a later plane to Detroit?"

And that's what I did. It was my first introduction both to typical American spontaneous hospitality, and to Studs. Breakfast, I remember, was oysters and Wild Turkey whiskey and coffee, so it was a memorable meal. He and his wife Ida were both absolutely delightful and kind to me, a complete stranger: and Studs said why didn't I come back to Chicago after Detroit for a couple of days, because the big Democratic Convention was going to be held there, and it would be an experience for me to see at least a part of it.

That was what I did, and I met James Cameron there who was covering the convention: and Studs and he and some of their friends gave a party at the hotel we were staying at. I don't know if you recall the occasion, but it was the famous, or rather infamous, convention at which things turned very nasty. There was fighting and rioting, and the National Guard were called out on to the street near where we were. At times the hotel resembled a frontline first-aid station. So that was another introduction for me—to a very different side of America than Studs and Ida had shown me, and a very ugly one too.

About two or three years later I went actually to Chicago itself when I was invited to lecture at the School of Architecture at the university there, and Studs interviewed me for his radio program. He astounded me by how much he already knew about architecture himself. One thing was very funny, I remember: he rather mischievously asked me what I thought when I saw the new buildings they'd recently put up as an extension at the university. I said facetiously, and completely jokingly, that I didn't like them much, they looked as though they'd been designed by a repressed fascist psychopath. The program was recorded and didn't go out until a few days later, by which time I was safely back in England: but apparently someone at the university heard it. And you know strangely enough I've never been asked to go back there again, I can't think why.

Over the years, Eleanor and I have got to know Studs really well, and whenever we're in America or he's in England—which unfortunately isn't too often nowadays—we always have at least one meal together. He once interviewed me here with his tape recorder, or no I think it might have been twice, but whether he ever used the interviews on his radio program back in Chicago I don't really know.

Naturally, as you can imagine, I'm not the sort of person who gets interviewed very often—why should I be, I'm not a stage personality or anything? But I must say that for an inexperienced person like me, Studs really does make it very easy. He has a great knack of putting you at your ease by making you feel he really wants to hear about and understand your point of view—and this very quickly conveys to you a reciprocal feeling that *you* want *him* to understand it, and will try as hard as you possibly can to help him do it. Quite how he achieves it I don't know, but he unfailingly does. I think it's partly because you trust him implicitly, you know he's not going to try and make you sound stupid: and in fact he quite often makes you feel when you think about it afterwards, or he does me at least, that I'm actually really more articulate than I thought I was. He has this gift too of conveying to you you're helping *him* along in his understanding of something, and that of course always makes you feel good.

Also he never interrupts, which I think is very important. Even in ordinary conversation when people do that to you, after a while if they do it too often you begin to feel they're not so much wanting to hear your point of view as give you theirs. The very opposite is true with Studs: he wants to hear your point of view, and he wants you to express it first in this way and then again in that way if you feel that's a better way of putting it, and then a third time after that if you're still not happy that you've made yourself clear. A great gift, you know, and I often think a lot of interviewers could learn a lot not only from listening to Studs asking people questions, but from listening to Studs listening to people.

Both he and Ida mean a very great deal to us, and their friendship's always brought us great enjoyment.

Joan Littlewood, Theatre Director

—My God isn't it hot, I'd no idea it could ever be so hot in England. I've only come here yesterday from Avranches but that was near the sea so it wasn't so bad. But even when I was in Sydney Australia last year in the height of their summer it was nothing like it's here in London now. I mean I feel I can't breathe properly, still I suppose I'll get used to it.

Yes well Studs Terkel you want to talk about don't you? I think I'll sit in this chair near the door to the balcony where I can feel the breeze, will you be all right in that one by the table there? No, I'll tell you what, I'll sit at the end of the table next to you and then we shan't be so far away from each other and we won't have to shout. Haven't they got a lovely garden, so green and cool looking and those splendid trees, limes I think they are aren't they? John's gone out to get a few salady things for our lunch, he says he does hope that'll be all right for us, it will won't it, I'm not a big eater in hot weather like this are you?

In the high-windowed bed-sitting room on the ground floor at the back of her friend's ground-floor flat in south London, she squeezed herself in between the table and the wall and moved a small pile of papers and books to one side to make space to rest her forearms on. She picked up a sealed envelope with a flourishingly handwritten address.

—Oh damn, look what I've found, I forgot to ask John to take it with him and post it for me. Would you put it in a letter box for me when you go, would you mind? I've put the same postage on it as I would for a letter anywhere in England, now we're all in this European Union thing I think we're all the same aren't we for the amount? I suppose I shouldn't have put "Holland" on it though really should I, I ought to have put "Netherlands"? Still I expect it'll get there just the same won't it, the post office people'll know?

Studs Terkel, well I don't know there's all that much I can think of to tell you. Pardon? What occupation should you describe me as having at the head of my piece? Well I really don't mind, call me what you like. Oh no, not "theatre director," definitely not, no not that. No, not "former theatre director" either, that'd be something I wouldn't like at all. It's the word "director" I object to, all theatre directors in my opinion are puffed-up illiterate bums like, well, like Laurence Olivier was, camping it up in *Othello* with a rose and all that sort of nonsense, or people like Peter Hall. The word makes me absolutely shudder.

When I was a child you know, even as young as eleven, I learned the whole of Shakespeare, I could pour it out. I did, too, everywhere, at school, at home, I was absolutely fascinated by the words: I don't think people pay enough attention nowadays to just the plain simple words he wrote. That's why I wouldn't want to be allied in other people's minds with the sort of people who do that.

And if it was *"Former* Theatre Director" they'd think of me as, well, as having been in residence in one of those dreadful buildings in New York or London or Paris or Moscow or anywhere. In China you know people perform plays in the open air, on platforms in the streets, or on trolleys. Seeing them do that taught me what theatre was really about, or should be. It was like religion you know, all-embracing, finding the God in each child and the whole meaning of joie de vivre.

Studs Terkel . . . Of course I write as well, but I wouldn't like to be called "Joan Littlewood, writer." I don't mean anything personally by it but I think on the whole, people who call themselves writers are phonies. Look at England for instance, what real writers have we ever truly had since Laurence Sterne, and God when did he bring out *Tristram Shandy,* it was about the 1760s or something wasn't it?

If I absolutely had to describe myself I suppose I'd say that for years now I haven't been anything really, not much more than a wanderer I suppose. I don't have a home, I don't belong anywhere: ever since my partner Gerry Raffles who I lived with since I was a girl died, I've never had a home because he was the love of my life and wherever he was, that was home. In the ten years since I lost him I've just gone around wasting my life without any enthusiasm or purpose. I suppose now I should just be called "Joan Littlewood, vagabond."

But I'm still at heart fundamentally a saboteur, so you could put me down as "Joan Littlewood, vagabond and saboteur." That would be fairly accurate. Michael Billington once wrote in *The Guardian* that I was what the French call in the film world an *animateur,* so that'd be all right. Oh and Ken Tynan once said about me "She doesn't direct a play: she creates theatre." So you can take your pick, but really I don't mind at all what you call me, it's up to you.

Don't let's talk about me though, you want to hear about Studs don't you and how I met him and things like that? I don't know you know, it's not all that comfortable here like this, I think I'll push the table a bit further away from me: will you give it a little bit of a pull at your end?

Thanks. Well now. I didn't know Studs Terkel from Adam, and one night when we were playing on Broadway in New York, or maybe it was just off Broadway, I don't know how they define these things, I was sitting in the little dressing room I had backstage, writing up some notes like I always do to remind myself of things I've noticed while the performance was going on, and there was a knock on the door and it opened and in breezed this big smile with this lovely fella behind it. We immediately started chatting about the play, and it was obvious from the way he was talking he'd already seen it at least once before that time, and was already really quite familiar with it.

He started asking me very perceptive questions about different points in it, and I soon found myself talking and totally at ease with him. After only just a few minutes he took a tape recorder out of his pocket and he said "You don't mind do you?" and he switched it on while we went on talking. I didn't mind, and it was all done so normally and naturally I thought he was just a newspaper reporter or someone like that. Anyway I'm a great casual talker to anyone: even if we've only just met I'll chat with everybody everywhere any time—except Peter Hall, I wouldn't talk to him or those others who're what're supposed to be the "right sort" of people—and I should think it only took about twenty minutes for me to be talking to Studs as though he'd been my best friend all my life. And I still didn't know who he was, and not even his name even.

I don't know what the reason was for him being in New York, but he and his wife took Gerry and me out for a meal, and not long after that they came to London and we did the same with them. Whether he ever used the interview he'd recorded with me on his radio program in Chicago I don't know: but we did once go there and stay with them for a few days, and Studs took us around and showed us the lake and all the parts of old Chicago which he loved and which were gradually disappearing as new buildings were put up. And he took us to some jazz clubs because jazz is one of his great passions. He seemed to know everybody and obviously there he's well known and everybody is very fond of him, which nobody can help being once they get to know him. Just being with him, if you're depressed or moody about anything you don't stay that way for long: he's like a sudden burst of sunshine on a rainy day. I've no reason for going to America these days, and I often wish I had, just to see him again.

And I'm afraid that's about all I can think of about Studs. I don't seem to have had much to tell you, but then I said I didn't think I would have didn't I? Oh good, that sounds like John coming back, I hope he's brought something good for our lunch: oh and don't forget this letter you said you'd post for me will you? What? Oh, didn't I say? It was *Oh, What a Lovely War!*

Lady Moni Forman

The widow of James Cameron, the distinguished journalist and writer who died in 1985, she is now the wife of Sir Denis Forman, the former Chairman of Granada Television.

—I came to know Studs through my late husband James, who'd met him I think sometime in the midsixties. James was the first Western journalist ever to be allowed into Vietnam to meet Ho Chi Minh, and his interview with him was published in *The New York Times*. It caused an absolute uproar in the States because there was great hostility there towards Ho, and that anybody should actually report what he'd said was considered absolutely outrageous, America and Vietnam being still at war.

James was returning via New York to England because he had a couple of other things he wanted to do, and his visit coincided with his article's appearance. Some television talk-show hosts found out, and persuaded James to be on their programs. One of them, without any warning at all, absolutely savaged James and he was so distressed by the experience that when he went back to his hotel room afterwards, he told me he felt so alone and friendless in a big city where he knew no one, he just sat on his bed and wept.

The next morning he had a phone call from Studs Terkel, whose name meant nothing to him, who'd apparently seen the show the night before. He said he was briefly in New York and could they meet for a coffee or something. Which they did, and Studs could see how upset James was, and he said to him why didn't he come back to Chicago with him, which was only an hour's flight away, and record another interview. This would be for his daily radio show, and Studs promised he'd give him plenty of time and a completely fair hearing.

He was as good as his word, and asked him a lot about his work and about Ho Chi Minh, who after all was the leader of a country of over twenty million people: and James always said afterwards it was a very healing experience for him and made him feel his work was worthwhile again. As a result he always afterwards had a great affection and respect for Studs. Studs did too for James. In many ways they had very similar characters, and they became really close friends. In due course Studs came to England, and I met him and his wife, and we've been there to Chicago to stay with them. At one time James was invited by an American university in Portland, Oregon, to stay there for three months as a writer in residence. While we were there Studs and Ida came to stay with us for a week, and he and James gave some lectures together to the students and did some question-and-answer sessions as well. It was a very happy experience, and my two grown-up children still go over to Chicago to stay with the Terkels sometimes.

One of the proudest moments of James's life, I know, was when Studs dedicated his book which won a Pulitzer Prize, *"The Good War,"* to him. The dedication reads "For James Cameron, master of his trade" and James was quite overcome about it. It wasn't only that Studs should have done it, but also that he should have chosen so precisely the very words as those he used. James always insisted that journalism was not a profession, it was a craft or a trade. He said a profession was something that had a set of rules that everyone engaged in it abided by, there were certain regulations which controlled the practise of it, and there were different levels which you took examinations for, and you gained or failed to gain accepted standards of achievement. You couldn't be a doctor or a lawyer or a teacher, for example, unless you were recognized in this way. But a journalist was more like a barrel maker, say, or a worker in wood or something like that: you might be a bad one or a very good one, but if you were a good one it was because you practised a trade. You were a craftsman, who never stopped learning how to be better at it. He must have said this to Studs some time, and it stuck in Studs' mind and that's why he so carefully chose those words.

Another outstanding thing about Studs, to me, is what a really good friend he is to so many people, and not just a fair-weather one. When I used to travel around quite a lot with James and we stayed at Studs' and Ida's house, one of the people we often used to meet there was Nelson Algren, who years ago when he'd been younger had written a book called *The Man with the Golden Arm.* When it first came out it was very popular: it was made into a film with big-star names in it, and Nelson had been what they call "much sought after." But that was twenty years before, and ever since then his career had more or less disintegrated and he'd written a few magazine pieces but nothing much else.

He was a great friend of the Terkels, and as I say, he was quite often there for the evening or just having a meal or a drink. Nothing ever seemed to come off for him any more, and he wasn't exactly embittered but he wasn't the brightest and jolliest of company, he was always morose and sad. But Studs was always marvellous with him, laughing at his jokes, good-humored and supportive and always telling him things looked as though they were about to get better for him. Nelson could be very sharp-tongued and sarcastic about people, and he really made me wince sometimes with some of the unkind things he said about people, even ones we'd not even met. But Studs would always turn them off with a laugh, and if it was something particularly outrageous he'd say "You don't really mean that Nelson, you're just saying it to try and shock us, that's all." And then when Nelson'd gone he'd say "Oh isn't Nelson witty?" or "Isn't he funny?" and tell us what a great writer he was or something brilliantly clever he'd said last week, and how terrible it was people just didn't recognize his talent.

I mean I've read Nelson Algren's work, or most of it, and though he's all right I wouldn't say he was quite the towering literary figure Studs still makes him out to be even though he's been dead now ten years or more I suppose. But this is the point I'm making about Studs: once he's your friend, you can rest assured he's your friend for life.

And I always think he has the perfect partner in Ida. I don't mean he doesn't keep friendships going and leaves it to her, but she's deeply involved in them with him too, and takes the initiative herself very often about keeping in touch. I think they probably tell each other every day who they've spoken to when they weren't together. She phones me, or I phone her, regularly once a month and we always find lots to talk about. She always enquires about the children, what they're doing and where they are, and she talks to Denis if I'm not here, he's got to know them well as well.

She's a gorgeous person, so tiny and slight like a ballet dancer, and she trips around almost as though she's on tiptoe all the time. But underneath that there's a very tough little person indeed. If we're out somewhere and after a while she's getting tired and wants to get home, she just raises that soft voice of hers a little above the general chatter and says with a smile "Louis dear"—she always calls him "Louis," never "Studs"—"Louis dear, I think it's time we were getting along." And he never ignores it or pretends he can't hear, he just straight away asks for the bill or whatever and starts the goodbyes. They've an amazing rapport.

Oh I could, I could go on talking about them for ages.

Mike Dibb, Television Producer

He lives in a tall slender terraced house in a mews in west London. We talked in his tiny workroom-office on the top floor.

—I'd never met him, but I'd read several of his books and liked them, and one day the program chief of *Arena* at the BBC where I worked asked me would I like to do a film about Studs Terkel? Usually you tend to think up your own ideas: that was the first time I'd ever been taken very much with someone else's, and I immediately leapt at the chance, especially as there were no limitations about how to do it, except the budget. It was left entirely to me what it should contain and how it should be done, so long as it was all kept to Chicago.

When I phoned Studs and asked him about doing it, he seemed very pleased, and we settled what dates he'd be available at a time a few months ahead. I phoned him a few more times to check on details, and it went very smoothly all the way. I can't think of anyone I've ever dealt with who was more friendly and cooperative and easygoing, and this was before we'd even met.

In due course I laid on the BBC camera crew and sound recordists. Then when the date arrived I went to Chicago a couple of days ahead of them to meet Studs and we sketched out a rough plan for the three weeks we'd be working together, and I looked at some locations for us to do our filming in. I wanted it to be as spontaneous looking and improvised as possible, so we didn't rehearse questions: and Studs phoned around a few people to see if they were in town and would be willing to take part in the program as well.

By the time the film crew arrived I knew I was going to have easily as much or more material as I wanted, and after they'd rested for a day or so we plunged into work. Most of the filming was done at the offices of WFMT, the radio station in the big modern office-tower block where he works in downtown Chicago at East Wacker Drive overlooking the river. All the staff there were tremendously friendly and just as helpful to us as he was. We filmed him interviewing people on his radio program, and him working in the archives of the enormous tape-recordings library of his work which they have.

We did a lot away from his office too, because his gregariousness is something I also wanted to show: we filmed him with friends and colleagues in restaurants, talking to people in the streets, and sometimes at his home as well. His wife Ida sometimes appeared there too or joined him for a meal: although she was always very warm and friendly and hospitable to us all, she wouldn't ever agree to be interviewed, apparently she never does.

Studs introduced us to several other people who would and do though. One was Vernon Jarrett, the black editor of the Chicago newspaper for black people called *The Defender,* another was a prominent civil rights activist whose name I'm ashamed to say I've temporarily forgotten, and a Polish steelworker he was friendly with, and he took us several evenings to different jazz clubs where we talked to pianists and saxophonists and filmed them playing.

He himself was wonderfully entertaining company to be with, and it's always amused me that here's this man who's supposed to be—well he's not only supposed to be, he *is* one of the greatest interviewers and listeners in the world—and when he's not working, by which I mean when he's not interviewing—he never stops talking! Talking, talking, talking, in a great cascade of words. Always very entertainingly of course, even though if you're in his company as I was for several weeks at a time you begin to notice him saying the same things, or telling the same stories repeatedly and in more or less exactly the same words. But then at his age who wouldn't? I know I do it myself quite often and I'm nothing like as old as he is. I sometimes think he's got a sort of filing system of tape recordings in his mind, and there are certain trigger words that when he hears them, he slots a cassette into his brain and out comes what he has to say.

But when he's interviewing, he has no trouble at all in listening and taking interest in whoever it is who he's talking to, and he does no more than put in the very occasional prompting question. I know I couldn't do it, especially if it was with someone I really found so objectionable I couldn't stand them. I asked him about one of the interviews he'd done which I'd read in one of his books, with a Ku Klux Klansman: I said to him something like "How could you possibly talk to someone like that, without wanting to argue with him or at least turn your back on him and walk away?" And he was really surprised. He said "But I couldn't understand him, I couldn't understand how anybody could think like he did and not even be aware I could possibly be offended by what he was saying. I was fascinated and I got really hooked on trying to find out." And it was true, he meant it: and then he said to me, and he really meant this too, he said "And you know, underneath and at heart he was a really nice guy."

I think he does think most people are fundamentally decent, and if they're not he tries his hardest to find out the reason why they became like they are: and it's often with startling results. He's fond of saying that he thinks of himself as being like a gold prospector—he's searching for gold, and he might have to sift through mounds of dross and mud and rubble to find just a few grains of it, but it always gives him great excitement if he does. I think too that he's ideally placed as an American to have an almost limitless terrain of characters to explore: he really loves the ethnic diversity of the American people and how different they all are.

Although I couldn't say I know him very well, I've always felt a special affinity with him because of what got me reading his books in the first place. I was working for the BBC, not long after I'd started with them, and Studs Terkel came to England for some reason or another and I heard an interview with him. I didn't know who he was, but he was talking about one of his favorite subjects, which is how wonderful it would have been if they'd had tape recorders in ancient Egypt, and today we could hear the actual voices of the slaves who labored to build the pyramids. And in extension of what he was saying, he quoted the first few lines of a poem by Bertolt Brecht called "Questions from a Worker Who Reads" which go something like:

> Who built Thebes of the seven gates?
> In the books you will find the names of kings.
> Did the kings haul up the lumps of rocks?
> And Babylon, many times demolished
> Who raised it up so many times?

And so on, but I don't remember the rest by heart. What so startled me though was that that poem was almost a personal talisman of mine—so much so that I had a typed-out copy of it pinned up on the wall in front of me at my desk. And here was this man I'd never met and up till then never even heard of, reciting it! Unfortunately the program was recorded, so there was no chance of dashing round the building looking for him. But that's what sent me out straight away looking for his books.

8

Themes and Dedications

GIANTS OF JAZZ. Crowell, 1957; reprinted 1975. (To John Lewellyn)

DIVISION STREET: AMERICA. Pantheon, 1967. (To the memory of Ring Lardner, Louis Sullivan, and Jane Addams)

HARD TIMES. Pantheon, 1970. (For my wife, my son and my editor)

WORKING. Pantheon, 1972. (For Jude Fawley; for Ida, who shares his vision; for Annie, who didn't)

TALKING TO MYSELF. Pantheon, 1977. (Remembering the hall room boys)

AMERICAN DREAMS. Pantheon, 1980. (For Nelson Algren)

"THE GOOD WAR." Pantheon, 1984. (For James Cameron, master of his trade)

CHICAGO. Pantheon, 1986. (For Ray Nordstrand and Norm Pellegrini)

THE GREAT DIVIDE. Pantheon, 1988. (To Lucky Miller)

RACE. The New Press, 1992. (Remembering Cathy Zmuda)

COMING OF AGE. The New Press, 1995. (To those old ones who have never ceased in the fight against the dying of the light)

—A bibliography sort of a thing? All my books in order of publication, what year they were published and all that stuff? *And* who they were dedicated to, why they were dedicated to them, all that as well? You want to know all that? Well OK let's try it and see how it goes: it's up to you. Do you have a list to remind me of the order they were published? Yeah I thought you might. You're sure one of those organized types of guys like Linda said. OK . . . go ahead.

Giants of Jazz. That was the first one, yeah. Came out forty years ago now. I believe I dedicated it to a man called John Lewellyn. He was the guy I originally wrote some of the pieces in it for. They were about different jazz musicians, I did them for a publication he ran. I wrote them for youngsters, you know, teenagers, to convey some of my enthusiasm to them. And you know something? I haven't seen that book around for years now. It's been out of print a long time, and I don't believe I even have one myself. It was reprinted too one time, about twenty years ago. If I have one I'll give it to you: remind me. Tell you the truth, I've almost forgotten what the damn thing looks like.

(Chicago Historical Bookworks of Evanston, a suburb of Chicago, said "occasionally but not often" they had for sale a secondhand copy of it. When they did it was what they described as "always a seventy-five to a hundred dollar book." I'd almost given up all thought of ever actually seeing one. Then one day I was chatting with Nancy Newman several months after the conversation with Studs and happened to mention it and my faded hopes. She said offhandedly "Oh I've got one" and took a copy down, in almost brand-new condition, from a bookshelf in her flat. Studs had inscribed and given it to her when it was published. Nancy let me turn its pages for half an hour before putting it back in the bookshelf and giving me a cup of coffee.)

Division Street: America. My first book in a sense, yeah, and ten years after *Giants of Jazz.* I didn't think of myself as a writer, you see, I thought of myself as a disc-jockey and a radio interviewer. Two people were influential in making me change course. One was the English actress Eleanor Bron, and the other was my publisher André Schiffrin who was an editor with Pantheon at the time.

Eleanor I met when I interviewed her and some of the other members of a satirical English show called *The Establishment* that was performing in Chicago. She asked me had I ever thought of turning some of my radio interviews into a book, and I said no. It was true, it hadn't occurred to me. So she sowed the seed as it were.

And the other person of influence was André. He and Eleanor had been students at the same time at Cambridge University, and I guess she mentioned the idea, of a book of my interviews, to him. He'd already been thinking about it too, you know, turning the idea over in his mind. So not so long after she was here, he called me up from New York. He said they'd published a book of interviews by an anthropologist named Jan Myrdal, called *Report from a Chinese Village.* And he said how about me trying to do something like it with the inhabitants of a village in America, only a larger one, say some place like Chicago?

I thought he was crazy. I told him, I said, "Are you out of your mind?" He said in that quiet whispering sort of a voice he has, with that funny bit of an English accent, "Well maybe I am. But just think about it." Well the more I thought about it, the more the idea started to take a hold on me, so eventually with a lot of misgivings I started on it. At the beginning I tried to find a street or an area of Chicago which was popu-lated by a variety of different ethnic, racial, educational and income–background groups. But I failed: there isn't one, or at least I couldn't find one, so the book has interviews with people from different parts of the city.

Say, incidentally, there *is* a "Division Street" in Chicago, you know. Only the book's in no way related to it, the title's purely metaphorical. Do you know about the bridge there? There's a bridge over the river at Division Street and Halsted: on my eightieth birthday the city honored me by naming it "Studs Terkel Bridge." Boy, oh boy. The plaque has been lost or stolen.

The dedication? Remind me how it goes, the wording of it. "To the memory of Ring Lardner, Louis Sullivan, and Jane Addams." Well this was very much a Chicago book, you know what I mean? And those three people, they were three people who in their own different ways repre-sented different aspects of Chicago to me. They kind of imprinted me with Chicago, one way or another.

Ring Lardner, he was a sportswriter, a writer of short stories, particu-larly stories with a baseball or boxing background—two sports I was mad about when I was a young man. What Lardner wrote, and I'd say more importantly the *way* he wrote, it was literature. There's no other word for it. It's not easy to do with subjects like that. But Lardner did, he was a great writer, and I wanted to pay my respects to him for it.

The second guy, Louis Sullivan, he *was* Chicago. In a lot of ways he still is. He was an architect. He died in 1924, and he was known as the father of modernism in architecture, the father of the modern school. His principle was "form follows function." It was he more than anyone else who made the skyscraper America's best-known contribution to architecture. He had a tremendous influence on all his students, including Frank Lloyd Wright. Lloyd Wright used to call him his *lieber Meister*. What went wrong with his life at the end I don't know, but he died on skid row. Can you imagine that?

And Jane Addams, do you know about her? OK well I'll tell you. She was a social reformer, a leader in the suffragette movement, a pacifist, and a Nobel Prize winner in 1931. She was important to Chicago because it was here that she founded Hull House around the turn of the century. That was what you might say was a mission, a settlement for helping the poor and underprivileged in a run-down part of the city. You know where she got the idea from? It was after she'd visited London and been to Toynbee Hall. Later on she was one of the founders of the American Civil Liberties Union. At one stage in her life, in the 1920s she was described by the Daughters of the American Revolution as "the most dangerous woman in America today." She must have been quite a woman huh?

OK then, what comes next?

Hard Times. This one again was André Schiffrin's idea. All my books, all of them always have been from ideas André's come up with. There've been others he's had too, other ideas I mean, but they didn't catch hold with me. Then after a while he's put up another one, then if I didn't like that, another one, and another one and another one. Then suddenly pow, bingo! One sounds a bell and I think about it, and if it stays with me and won't go away finally I call him up and say "That's it André, that's the one I'm gonna do." Mind you, I'm wrong sometimes. It sticks a while and then it crumbles and there's nothing there and I think "Where the hell's it gone, why aren't I so keen on it anymore?" It was like that with the youth book I told you about a few years back. I was enthusiastic to do it at first, but after a while it disappeared.

But if it lasts OK, then he leaves me on my own to get on with it.

We've had that kind of partnership ever since we've first worked together, it's supported me all my writing life. It began as a working relationship, then it developed from that into close friendship. It's a kind of security for me.

The dedication's an easy one to remember for me. I don't have to find a copy to remind myself of it. It says the book's for "my wife, my son and my editor." That's because they were then, and they still are now, the three most important people in my life. Those words say it all, don't they, they're simple and clear enough?

That's right, this one followed much quicker after its predecessor *Division Street* than that one after *Giants of Jazz*. Three years as opposed to ten, yeah. The reason? Well when I was doing *Division Street,* I didn't think of myself as a book writer. But when it was published, well it attracted a fair amount of attention and more than its fair share of praise. And that did something to me. It gave me more confidence about what I was doing: it made me feel I could produce something more substantial than radio interviews. A radio interview, you do it and it's gone: the voices are in the air and then they're no more. The ephemeralness, that's part of the attraction. But a book is forever. You have to think about what's going to be in it several times over—not just the content, but how you're going to use an interview and where. You start thinking like a jeweller who's making a necklace—polishing the stones, grading them, comparing them, matching them, arranging them in both their variety and their overall unity. And because you've had the previous experience of doing it once before, this time you know if you work at it you *can* do it, it *will* turn out. You have the confidence. So this time instead of taking you ten years, it takes you only three. You're not so scared. Does that make sense?

Working. Yeah, well this was the big one—in concept, in popularity, in how many copies it's sold over the years. A million or more, so they tell me. Again the idea was André's, and this time I didn't need much persuading about it. It fitted in mentally with an idea I'd had in my head a long while, one we've talked about before. You know, "Who built the pyramids?" Ask anyone that question and they say something like "Everybody knows who built the pyramids, it was the pharaohs, right?" Wrong. It was the pharaohs had the *idea* of building the pyramids, for their own aggrandizement, to try and immortalize themselves. They wanted to show generations to come what rich and powerful and splendid guys they were. But they didn't actually build the pyramids themselves: they got peasants and slaves to do the actual work. It was *they* built the pyramids, not the pharaohs. And because there weren't such marvelous things as tape recorders those days, nobody ever went around among the builders and asked them what it was like, how they did what they did, how they got those massive stone blocks arranged the way they were. I put Bertolt Brecht at the beginning of the book, his lines on the same theme . . .

> When the Chinese wall was built
> Where did the masons go for lunch?

So let's say I took the book as an opportunity to redress an imbalance, OK? Do something in the present that would have been terrific if other people had done it for their own times in the past.

What did I mean by the dedication? What does it say? "For Jude Fawley; for Ida, who shares his vision; for Annie, who didn't." Yeah well Jude Fawley is the main character in Thomas Hardy's *Jude the Obscure*: he's not a well-educated guy, but all his life he has this thirst for knowledge and education. He believes people can better themselves by reading and study, even if they come from humble backgrounds. Everybody is potentially university material, I suppose you could say that was his vision: he was an idealist. And Ida is my wife, and basically she's like that, she thinks that way too. "Annie"—well, that was my mother. She's dead now, and I guess I was being unfair to her in putting that in about her. I think maybe she did share Jude's vision but in a different kind of a way.

Talking to Myself. This was one I wanted to do because I felt time was catching up on me. I was sixty-five. I wanted to pull together some threads, do not a proper autobiography in the way people usually think of one, more a sort of memoir of different people I'd met at different points and in different places in my life. One or two of them were short pieces I'd already done for magazines like *Harper's* or *The Nation,* but I extended them or polished them up a little.

There's not much that you could say was personal in it. I don't feel that area's of great interest to other people, as well as trespassing into their lives. It's mainly about people I met and knew, and remember with affection.

Who were the outstanding ones? There were others I'd interviewed and liked but hadn't gone into books and hadn't gone into radio programs. I didn't want them to go missing from my life so I wrote about them instead . . . James Cameron, Joan Littlewood, Chief Albert Luthuli, Mahalia Jackson, Ivy Compton-Burnett, A. S. Neill the educator: I went to talk with him at his progressive school at Summerhill in Suffolk. He was a great Scottish educator, years ahead of his time. He said his school "began as an experiment and became a demonstration." They say he died thinking he'd achieved nothing. There were a host of others too: people I remembered from my childhood, some of the inhabitants of the rooming house and hotels my parents ran. That's what the dedication means—"Remembering the hall room boys"—they were the occupants there who had the best rooms, those on the first floor, what the English call "the ground floor," on the same level as the entrance hall.

It was true, the title, I *did* talk it, into a mike of a tape recorder. I felt that way was the most comfortable, I was more at ease with it than trying to write it or type the only way I know, the hunt-and-peck method.

There's a new edition of it André's just brought out with some new material: a sort of twenty-years-on backward glance at it. Somewhat slightly—I repeat, somewhat slightly—more autobiographical.

American Dreams. I did a lot of traveling for this one. Why I specially associate that with it I don't know. I can't drive a car, so I was reliant on other people to drive me around: they did, hundreds of miles, thousands more like. I must have had a dozen people who chauffeured me around for it at different times.

There was a lot of traveling in another sense too you know. In what you might call the open-endedness of the subject, know how I mean? Ask people to talk about their work, or their lack of it in the Depression years, and that's somehow a finite subject. You're giving them a starting point. But ask them what their dreams are or were, whether they've achieved them or not: that's much more taxing. For them *and* for you. You've got to be careful where you're treading, you've got to be patient, people are talking about intangible things.

Yet somehow you know it seemed to work just that little better each time with each person as I went along. Maybe I was becoming more confident, maybe that was it. Or maybe I enjoyed the interviewing so much. When I decided I'd enough to make a book out of them, you know what? I'd too many—about twice too many, almost enough to make not one book but two. I had to be very strict with myself about the editing and leave half of them out all together. You have to do that as an editor, discipline yourself: it's a constraint you learn, I guess, from working in radio. Every writer needs to have it, whatever form they're working in. Some don't have it, they regard everything they write as so precious not a word of it's to be lost. However much it hurts, if it's too much—put it in the trash can. To me, if you don't, that's the mark of the amateur. I still have that problem. Hell, don't we all? I've got a paragraph at the end of the introduction to my new book apologizing to those I've left out. Things don't change much do they?

There are two interviews in the book some people have expressed surprise about. I don't often go for actors and movie stars and such, because of the carapace of being "a personality" they always wrap around themselves. In this one they're Joan Crawford and Arnold Schwarzenegger. The way I looked at it was I had the opportunity, and they were amenable, so why not? You could say maybe I was a little unkind in presenting them the way I did, and maybe it's perhaps no justification to say, "Well, that's what they said . . . and like everybody else they have dreams too." But I don't know: maybe the book could have done without them. Maybe I shouldn't have included them . . . I don't know.

Why'd I dedicate it to Nelson Algren? Well, I'm glad I did. I'm sentimental. The book came out in 1980—and the following year, 1981, Nelson died. So before he went, he knew about it, he knew that I'd done that: and I was glad because Nelson, you see, he'd been my best friend.

He was an outstanding person in my life. No, he was *the* outstanding person in my life. I'm sorry you never met him. I'm sorry everybody never met him, not just because he wrote *The Man with the Golden Arm* which I guess is what he was most famous for, but because he was such a wonderful guy. His horses never came in, and he was a street-corner comic which is another way of saying he was a poet. And he may have been the funniest man around, ever—which is only again another way of saying he was the most serious man there ever was. You want to know about life and love? Read Nelson Algren. You want to know about anything or everything? Read Nelson Algren.*

"The Good War." The subtitle of it's *An Oral History of World War Two.* You know, that's something I've never been happy about, being called "an oral historian." It's too much kind of a grandiose term, I'm uncomfortable wearing it. It's got too much air of academe about it. Don't get me wrong, I've nothing against academics: but I don't consider that's my approach. My books aren't histories, they're memory books. It's difficult to explain.

A thing people often don't notice about this one, or if they do notice it they think it must be a mistake or something, is the title's in quotation marks. There's a reason for that, which is it *is* a quotation from someone in it. It was suggested for the book by someone. He felt like a lot of other people do, that there was something special about World War Two. Nearly all other wars in history were hard to justify, but that one wasn't: on all counts it was necessary, and therefore it was a good one. The Nazis had to be stopped, and because they joined in with them of their own volition, so did the Japanese as well.

The book started in my mind as a small project but it ended huge. Like its predecessor, it involved a lot of traveling, to see and talk to and listen to people with interesting stories. This was because I wanted to broaden out its theme: I didn't want it to be only about one point of view, I wanted as many different ones as I could get, so that meant following up on as many leads as I could.

It's dedicated to James Cameron—"master of his trade" I call him, which he was. We first met in the midsixties, somewhere around there: I tell a story about him in *Talking to Myself.* There was immediately a *rapport* between us. I admired his style and his attitude to his work, and I described him as a man who answered only to himself. Sometimes you'll hear people say they think a reporter or a journalist ought to be impartial and detached: James Cameron didn't hold with any of that. He had principles, he had a viewpoint, he made it clear he had: to me that was far more honest than pretending some affected kind of false detachment. I said in *Talking to Myself* something to the effect I thought he had

---

* An only partly fictionalized portrait of him, and their love affair, is in Simone de Beauvoir's *The Mandarins.*

the heart of the innocent, the eye of the experienced and the style of the master: that pretty well sums him up in my opinion. He was a great man and I'm proud to have known him.

I don't have any one special favorite among my books: some days I like them all, other days I don't like any of them. I guess most days my feelings towards them could best be described as ambivalent, because I can see their faults and failings all too clearly. Every single one of them, yeah.

Chicago. In some ways, this is an odd one out. It doesn't owe its existence to André Schiffrin, it doesn't have a dedication or a list of thanks and indebtedness, long or short, to other people for helping me with it. What it has is a dedication to Ray Nordstrand who's our president and general manager of WFMT, the radio station where I work, Norm Pellegrini the program director, and an Acknowledgment to one other person, Don Gold, who persuaded me to write it.

It could be said, it should be said, it's not so much my book alone as a combined effort between me and five professional Chicago photographers, to pay a kind of tribute to the city in words and pictures that complement one another. It's a homage to our hometown, let's put it that way. I'd written an article for a magazine, and it was Gold's idea to expand it this way and make it whatever I wanted—personal, historical, lyrical, whatever. I tried to keep it spontaneous, that was the main quality I wanted it to have. How can I put it? Like a jazz number, one point providing the setting-off point for another, a thought here, an improvisation there. Parts of it are about my childhood, about the rooming houses and hotels my parents had, parts about politics, and that's how it goes on. Objective, subjective, a bit of autobiography, something of everything.

What's the word I'm looking for? "Impressionistic," that's about the nearest I can get to describing it. The photographs, the pictures, the words—taken together, the range they cover tries to give an idea of the scent and feel and sound of the place. Scenes, portraits, buildings, people—the atrium at Marshall Fields, the streets where all the cars were buried under six feet of snow for three days in January 1967, the young Mike Royko, Nelson Algren in his shirtsleeves in the sunlight . . . everything that for me and the photographers was part of the image of Chicago.

It was a short book. It didn't take long to do it, about a year at the most, between when we first talked about it and when it was finished. To me particularly it was Nelson Algren's book, because to me he *was* Chicago: I put in as an afterword the new introduction I'd written, not long before, for the reissue of his classic on the subject, *Chicago: City on the Make.* He'd been dead two years by then, so that was a way left for to me to pay tribute to him. "A hard-boiled prose poem" someone called his book. I'd be happy to be part of that.

The Great Divide: Second Thoughts on the American Dream. I say in the introduction to this book in many ways I found it the hardest thing I've ever done. It's true, it was. People think or sometimes they say they think, the more you do the easier it gets: I've never found that so. It's not because of age or physical strain though: it's because each time you set yourself a standard a little bit higher, you know how I mean? You always feel you've got to make what you're doing not only *as good* as the previous one, but slightly better. You're scared somehow of the critic who's going to say "Yeah it's good OK, but it's not as good as the last one, the one before it."

I wanted it to show how things have changed: between one generation and the next, maybe perhaps let's say within two generations. Only I didn't want it to be a nostalgia thing, not a sentimental appeal about going back to "the good old days." Know what I mean? Nothing of that sort. They weren't too good, those "good old days": people try and kid themselves into seeing them like that, all in a rose-colored haze. I didn't want to produce something as simplistic as that. I wanted the emphasis to be on the changes people had noticed in their own lives and the lives of other people—some of them good, some of them not.

The book's kind of unusual for having a personal experience in it, one set in a dialogue form. A schoolteacher in a Pennsylvania town called me up one day to say she was using *Working* as a project-assignment book in class. Some small number of her students, backed by their parents, were objecting to what they called the "obscene" language used by one person I'd interviewed and they wouldn't do an assignment which meant using the words. Can you imagine that? So I made a visit to the school, talked to the pupils in the afternoon and the parents in the evening. I'm not claiming I won them over to my point of view, but I felt it was justified to include that account because it illustrated another kind of "divide" there is in our society. One between two attitudes, two ways of looking at things.

The book concludes with an interview with an elderly woman imprisoned for protesting a nuclear-arms base. At the beginning it carries a quote favoring "lack of objectivity" by James Cameron. It's dedicated to Lucky Miller. That's right, "to" not "for" you noticed that huh? He's a person I've known a long time, all his life, greatly respect and in time hope to get to know better. It's a message, sure. Does that cover that one?

Race. André and the owners of Pantheon had a disagreement, you may have read about it in the press. He left them and set up on his own, and along with several other of his authors I went with him. He'd done all my books since I began, he'd become a friend, I owed him, I couldn't have worked with anyone else.

This one has as its subtitle *How Blacks and Whites Think and Feel about the American Obsession:* the last word of that, "Obsession," is a very important one. A long time before I read someone, somewhere, I think he was a Swedish sociologist, he referred to the subject of race posing a perpetual dilemma, or a problem, for Americans. It never seemed to me that word was accurate: because a dilemma or a problem seems somehow to suggest something you can solve, rightly or wrongly, by making a choice. It might be a right choice or a wrong choice, but you can make it. I think Americans haven't ever done that: what they've done instead is worry at it like a dog with a bone, they've never got around to taking positive action, or if they have they've soon gone back on it.

I don't exclude myself from this. As far back as *Division Street,* the subject was one that was worrying me and concerning me. There are echoes and resonances from the early books that are evident in this one twenty-five years later. I went back and talked to some of the same people, and to their children, who're grown-up. Some have changed their attitudes and slightly shifted their ground, but others haven't. Most of the common prejudices are still alive and well. One of the deepest-rooted is the one people have that "Blacks don't want to work." Well you know in the center of Chicago, just over the street from my office building, when they advertised for laborers a few years ago to start in on the building of a new Sheraton hotel, nine thousand black men queued in biting cold weather from five o'clock in the morning for the just under one thousand manual-laboring jobs.

In a radio interview in St. Louis when the book was published I was asked about my own feelings, whether on the whole I was disheartened or encouraged by the material I'd found. I had to say the truth—which was I was both. I tell you, I was like an emotional yo-yo, sometimes up, sometimes down.

My long-time transcriber Cathy Zmuda, who'd worked on all my previous books, she died just when she was starting in on this one. So that's why I dedicated it for her.

A small point here I'd like to make: when I did *Division Street* twenty-five years earlier, I wasn't conscious then that in some ways—in lots of ways—it was going to be a kind of a prologue to this book *Race*. It was only after I'd done it, done *Race* I mean, that I saw in many ways that's what *Division Street* was. Sometimes I talked to the same characters again twenty-five years on in their life in *Race,* sometimes I talked to their children. In one instance I talked to a woman who was pregnant and then talked all those years afterwards to the child she subsequently bore.

Coming of Age. Yeah, well this is the last one. Well, not the last one, I mean the latest one. Once more I owe the title and the idea, like I do the others, to André: I had it in mind calling it *Rocking the Boat* at first, but he suggested *Coming of Age* which I think is much better. And I was going to subtitle it something like *Power, Passion and the Old.* Only he thought something more directly descriptive would be better. Now it's "The story of our century by those who've lived it." Another example, you see, of why he's always been so important to me. He sees how to state things plainly, where to, and when to, as well as how to.

All the people I've interviewed for the book are over seventy. In their different ways they've never ceased their fight against what Dylan Thomas described as "the dying of the light." He called on his dying father to "rage" against it, I think that was his word. My people do just that. Some of them do it with dignity, some of them with an inner peacefulness and calm. This was one which for once I didn't do a lot of traveling for: I took Chicago as my center, because again Chicago's a microcosm of the whole of America.

Oh yeah and there's another thing—only a little thing, but it's like the completing of a circle, rounding something off, giving it a symmetry which I'm quite pleased with. It's this. You remember I told you about the parthenogenesis it might be called, of my first book, *Division Street*? How it came from André's suggestion about doing something like a kind of anthropological study? Well *the* great modern American anthropologist was Margaret Mead right? And of all her writings, the book which brought her subject into the popular domain was *Coming of Age in Samoa*. So my title is just a kind of a little nod of acknowledgment in her direction too.

It's not dedicated to any specific individual or individuals, and I guess it's the only one of my books that isn't. That's because, simply, it's dedicated to everyone; it's summed up by the first speaker, an eighty-year-old who says "Think what's stored in each individual's mind. Think to yourself 'You've got a file that nobody else has. There'll be nobody like you ever again.' " Which says it all to me.

9

Attitudes

Not the Best Type of Boy: The FBI File

A National Resource: J. Kenneth Galbraith

Not the Best Type of Boy: The FBI File

At the end of World War II in 1945, relationships between America and Britain on the one hand, and the Soviet Union on the other, deteriorated rapidly. The period of hostility and distrust between them, which came to be known as "The Cold War," lasted for more than thirty years. Vestiges of it remain, and still bedevil attitudes today.

In 1950, trials for treason of State Department official Alger Hiss in America, and atomic scientist Klaus Fuchs in Great Britain, greatly contributed to public fear and suspicion in the West about the extent of communist infiltration into, and influence on, their governments.

After twenty years of Democratic supremacy, when the Republicans returned to power in the USA, with the election of former General Eisenhower as president in 1952, among their politicians were some who unscrupulously took the opportunity to enhance their own reputation and authority. Of these, one of the most widely known was Senator Joseph McCarthy. At the age of forty-four he set up and presided over a committee to investigate what he termed "un-American activities." It rapidly established for itself a reputation as a far-reaching tribunal seeking out and exposing those who were, or had at any time been, communists. From that point it proceeded similarly to uncover socialists, liberals, and liberal-minded thinkers—anyone, in fact, who had or had ever had what the philistine Senator McCarthy deemed any "un-American" thought or idea. In time it went further still: its enquiries included not just the original "suspects," but all their past and present friends, associates, and acquaintances, however slight those may have been.

At this distance in time afterwards, it sounds ludicrous. It was: but also, and alas, it wasn't. It became a black stain, ugly and insidious, at first slowly and then rapidly spreading through nearly all twentieth-century American life. Constant televised hearings and lengthy press reports, combined with lack of governmental restraint and total public inertia, gained the committee nationwide influence and power. It could summon before it, and cross-question without mercy, anyone its members wished: it demanded to know details of their present and past political activities, and forced revelations of their friends' names, their friends' views, their own views of their friends' views, and so on. An army of agents, investigators and informants formed and multiplied.

Almost the entire weight of the inquisitorial enquiry was brought to bear upon people working in or among the arts and media sections of society—writers, film makers, actors, radio and television broadcasters, and communicators of all kinds—in other words, those who were considered to be influencers and opinion formers. A few, but only a few, were brave enough to refuse to testify; and a few others who were questioned by the committee would give no names of friends or acquaintances to it. At the height of what by then was known as "McCarthyism" throughout the country, none afterwards was able to find employment in their chosen profession and had to do other work instead. Some emigrated, some disappeared, some broke lifelong relationships.

The committee employed thousands of FBI agents to travel the North American continental cities, investigating and reporting on every individual whose name had been mentioned to it. They collected a mass of information, some of it of value but most of it not—from interviews, old newspapers, and gossip in bars and cafés, about countless people of little or no importance, and of no threat whatsoever to the security of the nation. Facts, inaccuracies, rumors, smears and innuendos were assiduously noted and returned to Washington for filing and indexing.

Senator McCarthy's accusations grew wilder and spread wider. He accused the heads of the United States armed forces of "coddling communists," and eventually he and his methods were formally condemned in the Senate in 1954. As the number of his supporters dwindled, he finally declared President Eisenhower himself was "soft on communism," and thereafter completely lost all credibility. He died in 1957 at the age of forty-eight, but his spirit still lives on in some parts of America and Britain, even today. Terms such as "socialism" and even "liberalism" may often still be considered euphemistic, and those who profess to believe in them as attitudes or beliefs are for some reason regarded as slightly subversive or, at very least, somewhat unpatriotic.

. . .

Twenty years after the McCarthyite era, Studs Terkel writes lightheartedly about it in *Talking to Myself.*

"I had been visited by an FBI pair a number of times, especially in the 1950s. I'm confident they had a fairly rich dossier on me, because during the 30s and 40s I appeared at many 'subversive' gatherings and made quite a name for myself as an effective collection speaker. The Anti-Fascist Refugee Committee for aid to Spanish exiles in France and Morocco, and the Civil Rights Congress to name only two—and I had volubly supported Henry Wallace for president in 1948. And in that same year, incidentally, I was master of ceremonies at the celebration of Paul Robeson's birthday at the Chicago Opera House.

The FBI needed some gold stars, desperately. The more dossiers they gathered, the more stars on their report cards. Naturally, I sought a dossier for myself; and one as rich as possible. It was not for myself I wanted it. You understand that. It was for the good name of the FBI. I was, in a sense, a double agent.

The occasional FBI visits to my house were not always pleasant. With a sense of some shame, I say this. My wife, usually the most gracious of hostesses, was for some unaccountable reason inhospitable. There were at least two occasions I recall when she peremptorily showed them the door. But to the FBI she manifested—how can I say it?—contempt. I was, of course, terribly embarrassed. I myself was hospitable at all times. I seated them. I offered them choices of Scotch or bourbon. I had triple shots in mind. Invariably, they refused. Once, I suggested vodka, making it quite clear it was domestic. I thought I was quite amusing. At no time did our visitors laugh. Nor did my wife. I felt bad. I did so want to make them feel at home. I never succeeded."

The passage of Freedom of Information acts in 1966 and 1974 allowed American citizens to have copies of files indexed under their name which were in the possession of the FBI. In the mid 1970s Studs Terkel asked to see his, and more than a year later and only after two further promptings, they were sent to him, with a printed accompanying letter, which said:

> Certain pages of documents and portions thereof
> are withheld, based on exemptions pursuant to
> Title 5 United States Code Section 552 and 552a.
> One of the exemptions is the name or anything
> else which might reveal the identity of an agent
> or agents who had made any specific enquiry, or
> the identity or location of any informant who
> had furnished information to an agent.

They made up a 2¾-inch thick bundle of 503 pages—many of them duplicated or triplicated, most of them forms and questionnaires with single lines, or in some instances only single words, legible. Covering a period of more than sixty years, they contained details of his birth, the schools, educational establishments he had attended, the various addresses he and his parents had lived at, and included somewhere in the region of 146 reports, none dated, and the majority of them so vague as to be almost meaningless, of his activities from the age of twelve upwards.

(In the small selection of excerpts which follow, the different obliterated names of FBI agents are indicated by the phrase "Agent X" for the sake of readability, and the symbol "0—0" denotes the erased names of the different informants.)

> Agent X reports that enquiries have failed to produce any information about Terkel while he was at this school.

> Agent X reports an interview with 0—0 who was a pupil at 0—0 school at the same time as Terkel, in which 0—0 remembers nothing about him.

> Agent X reports that Terkel was a pupil of his at 0—0 school, and "was not particularly impressive."

Agent X reports that when interviewed at Chicago Law School, 0—0 who was at one time a tutor there states, "While it is true that Terkel worked diligently, I did not consider him any more than average. His appearance was somewhat sloppy, and I considered him to be not the best type of boy."

Agent X encloses a copy of Terkel's application for a fingerprint classifier at the Federal Bureau of Investigation in Washington.

Agent X enclosed a report on Terkel's behavior during his Army service at Camp 0—0. It is stated that he was popular with his fellow soldiers. There is also a unit commander's note at the foot of it reading, "Watch him!"

A National Resource: J. Kenneth Galbraith

"If Studs Terkel did not exist, some suitably qualified supernatural authority would have to intervene and invent him. And that would be a demanding task. For he is more than a writer—he is a national resource. Many write about presidents, but he gets to the deeper heart of our history and our national life."
(From a review by J. Kenneth Galbraith)

Galbraith, John Kenneth. Emeritus Professor of Economics, Harvard University. Born Ontario, Canada 1908. Married Catherine Atwater, 1937. Three sons. Educated Cambridge, England, and Universities of California, Tufts, Michigan, Moscow State. Economic Adviser to National Advisory Committee, 1941. Director of U.S. Strategic Bombing Survey, 1945. U.S. Ambassador to India, 1961–1963. Tutor, Harvard University, Assistant Professor of Economics, Princeton University. Lecturer, Economics, Harvard University. Retired 1975. Author of numerous books, including *The Great Crash* (1955), *The Affluent Society* (1958), *Indian Painting* (1968), *An Ambassador's Journal* (1969), *The Age of Uncertainty* (1977), *A Life in Our Times* (1981).

(From *Who's Who in America,* Reed Reference Publishing, 1993.)

STUDS TERKEL

The Littaur Centre
Harvard University
Cambridge, Massachusetts, U.S.A.

Dear Mr. Parker

I have your letter. And will give all possible help. Studs is a very worthy subject. Be in touch.

Faithfully. (Signed) John Kenneth Galbraith

Disconcertingly, he was six feet eight inches tall.

Even more disconcertingly, his answers were all swift, crisp and sparse, especially at first. Unless questions were formulated very carefully to avoid giving him the opportunity of doing so, he responded to them with no more than a yes or a no, leaving me floundering and trying hurriedly to think what my next question might be. His voice was deep and gruff, seeming at times almost dismissive. He gave the impression he had been asked everything I was asking at least twelve times before—which he probably had.

—No I can't recall how I first met him, I've no idea.
—It was many years ago.
—It was either in New York or Chicago, or it could have been here in Boston.
—I don't remember why we met.
—I think perhaps I gave a good review to one of his books and he wrote thanking me for it, and then we met later, some time after that.
—That was possibly the way it happened, but I can't be sure of it. It would have been twenty years ago now at least. No, it was more like thirty in fact.

—Oh yes he's interviewed me several times over the years on the radio when I've published a new book. And twice for two of his own books as well. The first was *"The Good War"*—in that one I talked to him about my work with the commission set up in 1945 by President Roosevelt to report on the effectiveness, or rather I should say the ineffectiveness, of the American and British bombing of Germany. Then last year he asked me could he come and interview me about being in my eighties for his new book which came out this year, about people who're over seventy and which I believe is called *Coming of Age.*

Being interviewed by him on the radio, and being interviewed by him for one of his books? Yes, they're completely different in every way. In his books, he takes out all his own questions almost entirely, so that the piece by the person he's interviewing reads like a monologue. But if he's interviewing that same person on the radio, he has a conversation with them. Often Studs has as much to say or more as the person he's talking to. So the two techniques are very different, and one of the many incredible things about him, you know, is that he's without doubt such a master of both.

Well no, I don't know that I can expand on that much really. Perhaps to say that as a radio interviewer he's aware, and helps you quickly become aware of it too, that a listener is more likely than not someone who just happens to have dropped in on a program, and doesn't know who the voice he or she is hearing belongs to. But if he or she doesn't find it interesting, fairly soon he or she'll turn the dial to listen to another station instead. Therefore you have to keep the discussion lively but not too deep, I mean moving along all the time. It has to be kept conversational, yes.

But when the interview is for one of his books, then the discussion's on a different level altogether. The pace is slower, no one else is listening, so you have much more time to think and reflect. Which is exactly what Studs wants you to do, to give him a text on which he can exercise another of his special skills afterwards. And that one is the most important one, which is editing. And it's one very few people indeed possess.

You can't say it of many people, but in a book you can rely on it that Studs will present a very intelligently edited version indeed of what you've said, taking out your repetitions, keeping an eye on your grammar, and if necessary omitting those passages that are the less interesting and irrelevant ones. All this is very important—critically important, I'd say. It requires a great deal of skill and ability on the part of the editor, and Studs possesses both those to a very high degree. A radio audience, you see, will hear what you say, but then probably forget it within an hour, or two hours at the most. But a reader of an interview in a book could well come back several times to what you've said in the interview, and even quote it perhaps.

So it's in his books that, in my opinion, Studs' greatest skill—that of the editor—shows through. And what also shines through as well is his high degree of responsibility in conveying exactly what it was you wanted to be conveyed. I've never once felt with him that he's misrepresented me. In fact, you know, I've always felt the opposite—he's improved and made clearer and more understandable the points I wanted to make.

I would say that on a personal level we're very good friends. We took to each other almost from our first meeting. I think some people find that a little strange. But the fact remains we have a basic similarity in our temperament, however unlikely it may sound that an ex-Harvard economist and a very wise and worldly Chicago journalist should be so similar to each other. But we are, particularly in one respect—we both enjoy being what might be described as "irritants."

Do you know the phrase that was coined—I believe it was by the newspaper magnate William Randolph Hearst? You've probably heard it—"A good newspaper should comfort the afflicted and afflict the comfortable." I think the principle's one Studs and I both strongly adhere to. We get a great deal of pleasure out of it, out of telling people the truth when they don't want to hear it. We enjoy controversy, and neither of us is at home accepting any of the usual clichés without question. Like me, he's attracted to new ideas and the thorough discussion and examination of old ones. He's particularly expert at extracting information from specialists, and not so much simplifying it as clarifying it and making it available to and understandable by the public. It's a great talent.

I can't recall one specific example for you, not immediately, no I'm sorry, I can't. What I would say in general though, is that whenever he's interviewed me, either on the radio about one of my books, or for one of his own, I've always felt that his sole purpose was to try and encourage me to develop my ideas clearly and put them across to as wide an audience as possible. He asks his questions so that he sounds what he undoubtedly is—genuinely interested in what you think and why you think it. And he wants other people—listeners or readers—to know about these things too, and take an interest in them themselves.

Oh yes, I'm aware that certain people—only one or two, and they should know better—have referred to him as "merely" a journalist and called him "a populist" and said other derogatory things of that nature about him and his work. In my opinion what they're saying is absolute rubbish, and not worth listening to. Of course he's a journalist: one of the finest there is or ever has been. And if being "a populist" means you bring to the attention of a wide audience things which people have given no thought to before, I can only say that as far as I'm concerned that's fine by me. I think Studs Terkel is one of the great figures of our time. OK?

As I was leaving, he put his hand on my shoulder.

—I thought your questions were good, he said. I'm glad you're doing a book about him.

10

And What Happened Then?

Interviewing an Interviewer

—Interviewing on radio, interviewing for books, which do you want we should start with? Either's OK with me, I don't mind. Radio? OK, radio, let's see how far we get.

Two kinds, right? The "Ah yes but" radio interviewer, and the "Tell me some more about that" interviewer. I'm in category two, same as you. That French word we were speaking of once, the one we don't have something with an equivalent meaning of in English. In French it has two meanings both together at the same time. What was it, "raconteur"? A "raconteur" is a teller of stories for public entertainment. I like that, it's a good description of what I am, I guess. It's also got another French meaning too—it means a guy who's garrulous, but we'll leave that out OK?

Here we go, we're on our way then. S. Terkel, Radio Raconteur.

I guess the first thing to say is to stress the difference isn't it, between the guy I'm interviewing for the radio and the guy I'm interviewing for a book? Heh and let me say here when I say "the guy" I mean "he or she." I'm not going to keep on saying "he or she" and "him or her" all the time. "The person"—how would that be, should I try and remember to say "the person" all the way through? Aw the hell with it, I'll just say "the guy."

Difference number one is the guy being interviewed on my radio show, he *wants* to be there, he might even be *glad* to be there. That's the first hurdle over, and he didn't even have to jump it. He's over the second one too, which is *I'm* glad he's there, so he didn't have to jump that one either. That's a whole new beginning from the situation of interviewing someone you might put in a book. Right away it establishes a communication-bridge between us.

OK, there's this guy and he's written a book, and I've read it, and I've enjoyed it, and it's interested me. So what's my job? My job's to interview him in a way that'll do several things. One, to interest an unknown number of unknown people, some of them like me and some of them very unlike me, and most of them at all points between, in this guy and his book in the same way it interested me. Two, it's got to try and do more than that—it's got to try and make them talk about the book to those of their friends who didn't hear the broadcast and so haven't even heard of the book. And three, I've got to make the author feel good about the conversation we're having about it.

Note I've changed a word here. I've changed the word "interview" to "conversation." That's deliberate, because of the connotations. I'm talking about the connotations in my mind. You go for a job, you get interviewed: that means you get asked questions, and you give answers. There are right answers and there are wrong answers, and how many you give of each affects your chances of getting the job. Or there's been a crime committed, and the cops come around to see you, they take you down the precinct station and they interview you. Questions and answers, questions and answers. Well, I don't want it to be like that. I want it to be like a conversation, and I want it to be entertaining and I want it to be enjoyable. To me, to the guy I'm talking with, and to all that audience of eavesdroppers out there who're overhearing it. That's exactly the atmosphere I want to try and create, that they're eavesdropping. They're excluded from the conversation, but I don't want them to feel that, I want them to feel they could join in if they wanted to.

An aside here. Do you have what's called "phone-ins" in your country, interviewers with studio guests, and listeners call in and put questions to them? The idea being the audience can take part and feel they're joining in? Tell me something—did you ever hear one that didn't sound phoney?

OK, back to the dialogue, back to the colloquy. That's the word I was looking for. The colloquy between me and the guy who's written the book. I want it to sound as natural as anything so unnatural can possibly sound, which is why I keep my questions in—to give the impression you're overhearing a conversation.

It's unnatural because it's got an imposed framework of an hour. They let me run over a little, by as much as ten minutes sometimes, because Steve who's our engineer is going to edit it down for length. But what I always try to remember—this is important—is that the guy who's written the book, *he's* edited it, and his publishers, *they've* edited it, so I'm not going to trespass on their work. The broadcast editing is on my talk with the guy only, not with anything else. Only it's got to be I've already done my editing—my own editing, that is, in another way. I've done it by making the choice in the first instance, haven't I, between who I'm going to have on the program to talk to and who I don't?

Politicians, I don't have any of those. And another set of people I don't find too easy—there are a few exceptions, but only a few—are actors, screen people. Most of them have got a carapace: I find that very difficult to get under. How can I put it, it's like they've got their makeup on all the time. I don't want to be cruel about this, or too generalizing— but if you make your living pretending to be a whole series of different people, after a while I guess you don't know yourself which one you really are. Most often that's the thing you hear an actor or actress say. When they're interviewed about some particular part they're playing, when the person talking to them asks them what they like about it they say "Well so much of it's really like me!" They're not lying, it's true— at that moment, at that time, it *is* like them! But if last year you were Doc Halliday, and this year you're Willie Loman, then who in hell *are* you?

OK where do we go from here now? Well how about back to the beginning and see what we've got? I'll move from the general to the particular right? I'll stick with the sample we've mostly been talking about, which is the guy who's written the book—and let's say he's some-one I don't know, it's his first book, or if it isn't it's his first book that I've interviewed him about. What's the first thing I do? I pay him respect. And how do I do that? I pay him respect by reading his book—and if he's written others before this one, by reading those too, or at least I have a look at them. You'd be surprised how many people don't do that elemen-tary thing. You can hear them on other talk shows, talking to authors whose books they haven't read! Can you believe that?

So that's the first thing right, I read the guy's book. And I like it, and I think it's an interesting book and I think it's a good book. Naturally I do, otherwise I wouldn't be talking to him.

And a good way to start, I've always found, is to get the guy to begin with reading something out of his own book. It's like asking him to wear his most comfortable slippers, the ones he puts on when he's indoors at home. They're *his* words, *he* wrote them, he's more familiar with them than anyone. And a good follow-up to that is to go straight in with the question "Was that an easy passage to write?" I'd say that's one of the few times when a question with a yes-or-no answer serves a real good purpose. More times than not he's going to say "No it wasn't," and he's going to be so relieved that somebody asked him that and didn't just take it for granted, it's going to be a big big help in getting him started on talking to you and telling you all about it. So in a kind of a way, what it means is they're talking about themselves but they're not talking about themselves. Asking them was it easy hasn't got the bleakness about it that "Is that autobiographical?" has, because the answer to that one's always going to be cagey, it's going to be "Well yes and no" and that's going nowhere.

I keep coming back to this point, you know, and wondering what's the best way of making it, that I think a good radio interview should always sound like a conversation, it should never sound like an inquisition. The point it finishes at should leave the listener feeling they'd have liked it to have gone on longer. This goes back to the feeling of wanting to read the book, making them interested to learn more—about the content, about the person who wrote it. There should be an excitement to it, an unfolding, a discovering of a little more and a little more and a—and then that's the point it ends at. The next "little more" is the one you hope they're going to want to find out for themselves.

What are you, if you're a radio interviewer? Well, we've already defined it as being one person in a two-handed conversation, one partner in a duet. I think you've got to remember though, that you're the less important one of the two. You're the facilitator, you're the person who has to help the other one put over what *he* wants to say, not what you want him to say.

And so then we come to the end, the wrap-up, the sign-off—which I think is always good if you can leave the audience with something to look forward to. Whenever it's appropriate, I like to use "And what are your plans now, what are you working on, what comes next?" I like that one as a finish.

It's the easy part of interviewing, is interviewing someone for the radio. You've got the form, the shape, and the engineer will see to the technical side of it. You've got your person to talk to also, and you know what he's going to talk about. So it's all straight down the line, and if you don't get it right the first time, you go back to the beginning and start over, do it all again.

But that's not how it is when you're interviewing for a book. That's not how it is when you're interviewing the uncelebrated person. You're Columbus, you're setting out onto the unknown sea. There are no maps, because no one's been there before. You're an explorer, a discoverer. It's exciting—and it's scary, it frightens you. It frightens the person you're going to interview too. Remember that. Where in the radio interview you start level in confidence, in knowing where you're going, in the one-to-one interview you start level in the unconfidence, in not knowing where you're going.

There aren't any rules. You do it your own way. You experiment. You try this, you try that. With one person one way's the best, with another person another. Stay loose, stay flexible. Think about your lead-in, about whether it's going to be into the person or into the subject. One I some-times use is "Tell me where I am, and who I'm talking to." That's quite a good one, because it lets me follow up. When they've said where we are "and you're talking to John Doe," I say "And who's John Doe?" And if they start telling you, well then you're on your way.

I don't know how a tape recorder works. Not even the simplest one that's ever been invented. And I don't mean the machinery inside it either, I mean all of it. I don't know how to open it, I don't know how to put in the cassette, which way up it goes, how to close the lid when it's in, which is the button to press to get it to start recording, which is the button to press to make it stop. None of it, I don't know any of it. Some people say to me "Why don't you learn?"

Asking me why I don't learn is missing the point. I don't learn be-cause I'm nervous of the machine. If I press the button and the wheels are going round and I can see the tape's moving, that doesn't make any difference, I'm still nervous because I don't know whether it's recording what's being said, or whether I'm recording over something else that's already there and losing that, or what.

Are you with me? What am I describing? I'm describing one of my biggest assets. Its name is ineptitude. Why's it an asset? Well, would you be frightened of a little old guy who wants to tape-record a conversation with you—*and he can't even work his tape recorder?* We won't go into what you might feel about him, but the one thing you wouldn't for sure feel is scared.

So it's a bonus. I'm not up there on Mount Olympus, I'm not the Messiah with the microphone, I'm just another human being. I don't want anyone to be in awe of me. I don't mind what they feel so long as it's not scared.

Sometimes that way I can get more out of it too. I don't overplay it, but I'll often accompany the fumbling around with a question. "Heh, can you tell me if I've got this OK now, is this thing working OK?" That helps to ease the tension. It might even bring a smile or a laugh. So what's being done by that is this: you're asking for help, making it into you-and-them-together on the same side against the machine. You can't pretend though, it's got to be genuine: no tricks, no deceits. You've really not got to know what you're doing. That's why I'm always going to stay that way. Blessed be the ignorant: they'll often get the breaks.

So now we come around to the questioning. The first thing I'd say to any interviewer is . . . "Listen." It's the second thing I'd say too, and the third, and the fourth. "Listen . . . listen . . . listen . . . listen." And if you do, people will talk. They'll *always* talk. Why? Because no one has ever listened to them before in all their lives. Perhaps they've not ever even listened to themselves. You don't have to agree with them or disagree with them, all of that's irrelevant. Don't push them, don't rush them, don't chase them or harass them with getting on to the next question. Take your time. Or no, let's put it the right way: let them take *their* time.

And I'll tell you something else you should always have in your mind, and remind yourself constantly about it—they're doing you a favor. This person you're talking to is entrusting you with their memories and their hopes, their realities and their dreams. So remember that, handle them carefully, they're holding out to you fragile things.

I'm thinking of two quotations. One of them's from James Joyce, the other one's from Thomas Hardy. James Joyce's is from *Portrait of the Artist as a Young Man,* I think. "Tell me about Anna Livia. . . ." How does it go? "Tell me about Anna Livia, I want to hear all about Anna Livia. We all know Anna Livia, tell me all, tell me now." Anna Livia—the River

Liffey running through Dublin, the river of life. Tell me about the river of life. The Thomas Hardy one, I'm not sure which of his books it's in. "This man's silence is wonderful to listen to."

So there we have our two basic texts for interviewers, don't we? Tell me about the river of life, and listen to the silence. I'd say listen and wait are the two essentials, with watch and be aware a close third. A laugh can be a cry of pain, and a silence can be a shout. And God knows how many different meanings there are to a smile. It's what a person says and how they say it, and where they're saying it to—to you, to themselves, to the past, the future, the outside world. Those are the basics.

If you've lost touch, or you're unsure of where you're at and how things stand, I think a "How?" or a "Why?" question can be very harmful and destructive: and hurtful too, too much of a jolt. I said when we talked about radio, this isn't an inquisition. It's an exploration, usually an exploration into the past. So I think the gentlest question is the best one. And the gentlest is "And what happened then?" Maybe you'll get an answer, maybe you'll get a shrug. And boy, what an answer that is! A shrug means I don't know—or I don't care—or I don't care to know—or what the hell does it matter anyway? But it's a signal, isn't it? And what does the signal say? It says "Shut up and keep still."

Interviewing? Easy? Ask me another one? Exciting? Ah, you're right on the button with that one. Is it exciting? I'll say it is, yes!

· · ·

—Why me? That's what they say, isn't it? Why me, why'd you want to talk to me, I'm not important? I like that, I like to hear it, it's a good start. The uncelebrated person—oh boy, how many of those have we missed! There weren't any guys around with tape recorders when they were building the pyramids, when they sailed the Spanish Armada, when they fought the battle of Waterloo. We've spoken of this before haven't we, yeah, about how much we've lost? Bertolt Brecht said it, in *Mother Courage* was it, "Who built Thebes"? What we've lost. We'll do the best we can, right, to make up for the epiphanic moments, the things that really mattered, that are gone forever. What was it like to be a certain person then? What's it like to be a certain person now? That's what I'm trying to capture. I'm looking for the uniqueness in each person. And I'm not looking for some such abstraction as *the* truth, because it doesn't exist. What I'm looking for is what is the truth for *them*.

The word I'm looking for is "curious." I don't have to stay curious, I *am* curious, about all of it, all the time. "Curiosity never killed this cat"—that's what I'd like as my epitaph. It won't kill me, no sir. I breathed it, it's what gave me life, the older I got the more curious I became. What's happening, what's going on, what's it like, what does it mean? They're big questions for everyone.

"Do you work to a framework?" they sometimes ask me? And sometimes I answer yes and sometimes I answer no. What I'm trying to put over is that there aren't any rules, each time's a new beginning, right? That's what's exciting about it. Isn't it, isn't that what's exciting about it? If it wasn't, then you'd be better working for a market research company so that at the end you could say "I asked a hundred people the same questions, and these are the results." It's the uncertainty, the not knowing where you're going that's the best part of it. People aren't boring. Interviewing people is discovering people, and one of the biggest thrills you can get is discovering that somebody who sounds boring isn't boring at all.

One thing I'll never do is write my questions down. I'll not do it because it's false and it's unnatural and it's not what you do when you're having a conversation and it'll make them feel—here's that word again—interrogated. I want them to talk about what they want to talk about in the way they want to talk about it, or not talk about it in the way they want to stay silent about it. I'll keep them to the theme—age or the Depression or work or whatever—but that's all.

How do you get someone started? I suppose that's the one people ask me most often. Where do you begin? Well, childhood's a good place sometimes, that'll often open the sluice gates. But you've got to think out the wording first if you're going to use it, it's got to be something that requires a bit of thought from them to answer it. "How was it when you were a kid?" I think that's quite a good one. I think it's better than something more simple like "Did you have a happy childhood?" which they can answer yes or no. I try not to use questions which can be answered that way, you know, with a yes or no. I try to use ones that'll lead to a follow-up. An example? OK, off the top of my head. "Do you like Chinese food?" "Yes." "Do you like Indian food?" "No." So where's that got you? Nowhere. What's better is "Which do you like better, Chinese food or Indian food?" Because whatever the answer is, even if it's "I don't like either of them" you're straight in then with your follow-up—"Why?"

And people's answers aren't always direct. So don't be admonishing about it. Accept it, and think about it afterwards. We've talked another time, haven't we, about silences and nods and shrugs and things of that kind? Well sometimes the indirect answer that the person *thinks* is the answer is more informative than the straight answer. I said to a guy once, he was a retired meat boner in a factory, and he was telling me how he started work there when he was thirteen, and he said something like "And I tell you, when I was eighteen, I was in charge of a whole production line." And the way he said it made me say "You sound like it surprised you, why was that?" And he said "Well, me!" So I let it go. Then he said it again about something else—"Well, me!" And a third time "Well, me!" I was young in those days, and I didn't realize what he was telling me—until he added two more words to it, and then I knew what it was. "Well, me—a darkie!"

People's questions too, they can be signals to you. If you can answer them, do. Demystify the experience in advance for them, if they ask you what you want to talk to them about. But they might be saying there's something *they'd* like to talk about, something they *hope* you're going to ask about, so ask them if there is. And the best part's the detail that comes out, that you couldn't imagine because you never knew it was there. Perhaps the person didn't know it was there either.

The questioning's important—but what's the most important is that it shouldn't *sound* like questioning. What time did you get up yesterday morning, what time did you go to bed, what did you do in between— none of that. So tell me, how was yesterday, that's the right way of doing it. Making it sound like you're having a conversation, not carrying on an inquisition, right? There's that word "inquisition" again. I'd say that to everyone and go on saying it—keep away from it, don't be the examiner, be the interested enquirer.

There was this black woman one time, I saw her standing in the street with two or three of her kids round her and she was looking in a shopwindow. And as I'm walking by, I look to see what it is she's looking at— and you know what? There's nothing in the window, she's looking in an empty shopwindow—looking at nothing. So naturally I'm curious—*naturally* I'm curious—so I say "Excuse me ma'am—but what are you looking at?" She doesn't seem to mind being spoken to by a stranger, and she doesn't turn her head around to see who's asking her or anything, and after a moment or so she says "Oh" she says, "Oh, dreams, I'm just looking at dreams." So I've got my tape recorder and I switch it on and I say "Good dreams, bad dreams . . . ?" And she starts to talk. Then she talks a little bit more, and a little bit more. And her kids are playing around her, and they can see I'm tape-recording what their mom is saying, and when she stops talking after eight, maybe ten minutes or so, one of them says "Heh mom, can we listen to what you said?" And I ask her if it's OK with her and she says yes, so I play it back and she listens to it too. And when it's over, she gives a little shake of her head and she looks at me, and she says "Well until I heard that, I never knew I felt that way." "I never knew I felt that way!" Isn't that incredible? The way I look at it, it's like being a gold prospector. You find this precious metal in people when you least expect it.

And the contrasts and the rewards, well those come in all different shapes and sizes. I remember one week I was in Pittsburgh, I'd gone there to get material for a series of interviews I was doing on how working people spent their days. I'd two introductions—one to a college lecturer and the other to a guy who worked in an auto plant and lived in a mobile home with his wife on the outskirts of a small town nearby.

I met him in a cheap diner, we had something to eat and then we sat outside on a bench under some trees because it was summer and warm. All I said to him was something like "Tell me about a typical working day for you, how it would begin." I don't remember now why I used those particular words: they felt right, I guess.

"OK sir" he said, "well I'll tell you. I have one of those little electric radio alarm clocks, and when it goes off and I hear the music playing, my wife's lying beside me and she's still asleep so I give her a kiss. That's routine you understand. Then I get out of bed and I go to the bathroom, and I wash and I comb my one hair and I clean my teeth and I shave. Routine again you understand. When I step out of the bathroom by this time the radio's woken my wife up, and she has a cup of coffee waiting for me. Some days I drink it, and some days I drink only a half of it. All depends on my mood you see. Then I get myself dressed and my wife makes me two pieces of toast. So I eat the two pieces of toast, but some days I only eat the one. All depends on my mood again you see. Then I kiss my wife again, that's more routine you understand. My wife gives me my lunch bucket, I get into my car and I set out to drive to the plant. And I've got to get there on time, because you see sir, if you get one minute late, they dock you for one whole hour. And well sir, between my home and the plant there's nine railroad tracks I have to cross—and at that time of morning there's a lot of freight trains go by. So if I get to any one of those tracks at just a half a minute off the wrong time, I have to wait maybe fifteen twenty minutes or so while a hundred cars go by. And that means I am late for my work." Well the way he told that to me, by the time he'd finished I'm sitting on the edge of the bench! So I thought boy, that's some way of getting a guy started, I'm going to use exactly those same words again tomorrow with the college professor.

Which I did. I said to him "Tell me about a typical working day for you, how it would begin?" You know what he said? He said "Well, a typical day would be I'd get up, have my breakfast, go to my class, and since it's Aristotle's *Poetics* we're studying, I'd talk about it." I said "You'd talk about it? What would you say?" He said "Oh this and that." And that was all I got out of him! That was it! Nothing!

I guess the guy who lived in the mobile home had spoiled me. You can't be too prepared for an interview, because you don't know what the person you're talking to's going to say. But you've got to be ready for anything—and I wasn't ready for the unloquacious professor. In a way it's like jazz, you've got to improvise. Have a skeletal framework, but be ready to improvise within that.

The third, and it's *the* most important part of the work, is the editing of the transcripts of the recorded material, the cutting and shaping of it into a readable result. The way I look at it is I suppose something like the way a sculptor looks at a block of stone: inside it there's a shape which he'll find and he'll reveal it by chipping away with a mallet and chisel. I've got a mountain of tapes, and somewhere inside them there's a book. But how do you cut without distorting the meaning? Well, you've got to be skillful and respectful, and you can reorder and rearrange to highlight, and you can juxtapose: but the one thing you can't do is invent, make up, have people say what they didn't say.

I work from transcripts, but all the way through I keep on playing back sections of each interview so I'll have a constant reminder in my head of how they sounded when they said what they said. The most painful choice to make always is not who you're going to have in the book, but who you're going to cut out. Sometimes it feels like casting a play—you've got four equally good people for one character—only in the case of a book it's four people representing one point of view. It's a tough decision to make.

Some things are easy to remove, like "ums" and "ers," or you think they're going to be until you listen to them and you realize that that's how that person talks, and if you take all of them out, you lose the reality of the speech pattern of that person. Or someone else'll have a habit of repeating phrases—"Yes, that's how it was, that's how it was," say—and you've got to watch out that you keep those.

And length too of course, that's another crucial thing. You might think what the person's saying is very interesting. It might be to you. But it's got to be interesting to the reader, so keep an eye on that. I want a reader to feel they'd like to hear more, so the principle I try and hold on to is when in doubt, cut.

From sixty pages of transcript I reduce to eight. I talk while I'm writing: I talk *what* I'm writing. That way I try and get the sound and the tempo and the rhythm. I take out nearly all my questions because I don't want to stand in the way between the reader and the person who's talking. People aren't boring. When you talk to them, they may have a monotonous voice and you think they sound boring. But when you see their words transcribed, they read great. Other times it's the other way round—they're lively when they talk, but it doesn't come out that way on the printed page. So you have to exercise care. Oh boy—interviewing—isn't it great?

II

Castellations:
Studs Talking (3)

—How did I get it, the name "Studs" you mean, the nickname? Well I'll tell you for one thing, I was given it and I know the why of it. But the how of it, how it stuck and hung on for the rest of my life, well that I don't know. In 1932 when I was what, twenty I guess, there was a novel came out written by a guy called James T. Farrell. Its main character was a guy named Studs Lonigan: he lived in a poor part of Chicago on the south side and he was a no-good. A drifter, and a braggart, and a drinker, and a great one for the ladies too, or leastways he thought he was. Oh yeah, and he was an Irish Catholic too. So naturally I identified with him because we had nothing in common, OK? I never stopped talking about what a fantastic character he was to all my buddies and everyone I hung around with, as long as they cared to listen to me, plus a good while afterwards too.

What was I doing? Recognizing in myself something that no one else could see but me? Fantasizing, hoping I could be like that myself? I don't know. I only know it got to the point folk started joshing me about it, saying things like "Uh-oh, here comes Studs" and all that kind of stuff. So it stuck—and I didn't mind. Maybe it gave me something of a macho air, or I thought it did, maybe that was it, I don't remember now. Farrell wrote two more books in quick succession about the same character— *The Young Manhood of Studs Lonigan* and *Judgment Day*—and how he dies young and in the gutter.

I couldn't say he was what it's fashionably called these days a role model for me. But there *was* a fashion in Chicago, I recall, in those times for people to like to be called after figures people had read of in books or seen in movies. Damon Runyon inspired a lot of them: if your real name happened to be Dave, let's say, then of course everyone'd know you as "Dave the Dude" after the guy in his stories. Now sometimes people think it's my real name. What a lot of them don't know is that it's become so common I feel it almost *is* my name. But there's one person won't have that ever, and it's good she reminds me of it. My wife Ida never calls me anything but "Louis."

Oh and yeah, one funny little thing here is this. It wasn't even Farrell's first-choice name for his Lonigan character, which was "William" I think. Sometimes I wonder why *he* made up the name "Studs" and where *he* got it from.

I wonder too sometimes—you remember that schoolteacher I was telling you about? I'm not so sure the works of James T. Farrell were exactly what he had in mind when he was telling us about the glories of English literature and inspiring us to get around to reading them. Nor my brother Meyer either. I think his thoughts were more along the lines of Francis Bacon, you know: "Reading maketh a full man"? Maybe, maybe not: reading's a habit gets instilled into you isn't it? Like Nelson Algren used to say, once you've got it you can't help yourself, you'll read anything, even matchbook covers.

He was a great guy you know was Nelson, did I ever mention that to you? Yes you're right, did I ever *not* mention it to you. He was never properly appreciated—you know, least of all by himself. He wrote the best book on Chicago there's ever been. *Chicago: City on the Make.* Did I ever tell you that? Yeah, but I only told you once, didn't I?

When McGraw put out a new edition of it a few years back they asked me to write a preface for it and I was proud to. I put it in at the end of the Chicago book too, which is where it belongs as well. I'm sad he died sad. Yet, you know, his sadness wasn't depression, it was the sadness of the clown, the guy who all along underneath everything knows it's all funny, you know how I mean? One time I was with him some place I remember, and a young woman came up to him, and she said "Mr. Algren, I feel I'm on the threshold of being a writer myself, could you give me some advice?" He looked at her a moment, very serious like this, then he said with a fatherly sort of a smile to her, he said "Young lady" he said, "That ain't no threshold you're standing at, it's a precipice." That was the kind of guy he was. "Turn around and run" he was saying—"or go ahead and throw yourself right in." If she wanted to take it as encouragement, she could: and if she was looking for a let out, he was giving her one.

I like people like that, I like writers like that, I like books like that—I guess what you'd call Mozartian. Whatever frame of mind you're in, somehow they go along with you and you with them. It's a big regret I have that there don't seem to be too many books these days you can do that with—or maybe it's a sign that your mind's not as active as it used to be, I don't know. Discoveries, they're always exciting of course, aren't they? Like stout Cortés when he stared at the Pacific for the first time, "and all his men looked at each other with a wild surmise, silent upon a peak in Darien." What *have* I found, what am I going to find—there's nothing like that moment, is there? I remember feeling it when I read James Joyce's *Portrait of the Artist as a Young Man* for the first time.

Yeah, to be honest it didn't stay with me when I went on to *Ulysses,* I didn't experience the same thing. What else have I read that I liked? *Look Homeward, Angel* by Thomas Wolfe; *Moby Dick*—that was a great book. . . . "Call me Ishmael"—what a fantastic opening sentence heh? What else, let me think. Feuchtwanger's *The Wandering Jew,* Thomas Mann's *Buddenbrooks,* nearly all of Dickens, I like his social conscience and awarenesses. But you know I think what somebody *hasn't* read is almost as revealing about them though. *War and Peace* I've never read— that's why I'm always trying to get them to run it as a serial at the radio station. *Remembrance of Things Past,* Marcel Proust, I haven't ever got around to reading that either, nothing by Flaubert. . . . I must be one of the most widely unread illiterates there is.

The more you read, the more you know there is that you want to read—that was what Meyer always used to say. And there's so much good stuff around, isn't there, there are so many people writing so many good things? "May you live in interesting times," is it the Chinese who say that? Well we do, we sure do. . . . Sometimes I feel like yelling out "Heh stop the deluge a minute will you, hold on, not so fast!"

I said something just then reminded me of something, what was it, it reminded me of something else I wanted to say. . . . Oh yeah, I know, putting on *War and Peace* on the radio as a serial. Not dramatizing it, I didn't mean that, I meant reading it as a serial, yeah. People write in to us, I guess it's the same in your country, they say they've always admired this or that, it's a great book and why don't we read it as a serial? But you know what I wonder? Why don't they write "I've never read *War and Peace* and somehow I don't think I ever will, but if you read it on the radio I'd listen to it"? Why don't they do that?

I guess no radio station would though, would they? It's all part of this great shibboleth that's taken over the media these days—press, radio, television—they call it "giving the public what it wants." "Oh they'd never stand for something like that" they say, "they haven't got the attention span." That's another buzz-word phrase too, "attention span." Everything's got to be reduced to bite-sized chunks, or else people can't take it in. People can't concentrate on anything for more than a minute or a minute and a half, they tell us. It's an insult. Who are they to say they know what people want and they're going to give it to them? They're trivializers, reducing everything to the lowest common denominator.

You see it most on the TV talk shows now. Those hosts who parade celebrities one after the other, giving them all equal value on the surface, but underneath they're devaluing all of them and giving them none. You remember that book by Hannah Arendt, I think it was the one she wrote about Eichmann, where she spoke about "the banality of evil"? Maybe that was the title she gave it too. "The banality of evil and its ordinariness": it was powerful stuff. But I reckon it's about time now someone wrote a book reversing the subject, and made it about "the evil of banality." Here and now, that's what we've got. "Ladies and gentlemen, please give a big welcome on our show tonight to our two big celebrities, Professor Albert Einstein and Miss Zsa Zsa Gabor!"

It's crept into our lives, it's everywhere, it seems like we're endlessly obsessed with things that don't really matter, that don't touch us. It's as if what we want to feel deeply about are only things that it doesn't matter if we feel deeply about them or not. What we *don't* want to feel deeply about are the things that *do* matter. Have you seen the papers today? The thing they're full of is Michael Jordan the retired basketball player coming out of retirement and going to resume playing for the Chicago Bulls again, or is he not? That's the content of all the front pages, plus all the sports pages, and some of the newspapers have got special twelve-page supplements on it as well! And it's all speculation—the guy hasn't even said yet what he's going to do! That's the big news. And ask any news editor how he justifies it, and he'll tell you "That's what the public wants to know about today, more than anything else in the world."

Yeah? So let me tell you what the public ought to want to know about—something else that *is* in the newspaper today, but in a report only that big, two inches high maybe, at the foot of a column at the bottom of around page seven or somewhere there. It's that tomorrow, for the first time in eighteen years in the state of Illinois, a couple of guys are going to be put to death by lethal injection in Joliot Prison. Well, it's news, but it's not news the public's all that interested to hear about, say the great panjandrums who're the editors. We'll print it so's no one can accuse us of suppressing it, but it's not trivial enough to be spread over twenty-eight pages like the Michael Jordan nonstory. It's Gresham's law isn't it? Only in our modern times it applies not to money but to thoughts and information—the worthless and useless drives out the good. I'm getting to sound like a cantankerous old conservative aren't I, huh? Oh boy, any minute now I'll be advocating a return to the good old days with its workhouses and poor laws and servants below stairs and children working as chimney sweeps.

Meyer, you know, my brother, he always used to say if you knew something was good and you got pleasure out of it, you had a duty to try and pass it on. He sure did that with me. After you asked me the other day what did I think he'd given me the most, it was that. That enjoyment, that enthusiasm for things, especially music and painting. He used to take me to concerts—I think I've told you this before—Beethoven, Mozart, Schubert—and I think that that was a seminal experience for me in more ways than one. Not only musically in the obvious sense, going out and making discoveries on my own—Satie, Bartók, and the rest. I don't forget the whole field of jazz either, which is something else I've never lost a feeling of excitement about.

Musical form and the writing of books, they're connected for me. I get the feeling sometimes putting a book together's something like constructing a symphony. How's it going to sound to the audience, how's it going to read? Right from the beginning you've got to shape it. First movement, second movement, book one, book two, book three. How are you going to start? Softly, quietly, with a whisper—or like Shostakovitch does sometimes, with a hell of a loud crash, discordant, attention getting? Or you bring in a theme here, let it disappear, then come back and combine with another. Here it's solemn and heavy, there it's dancing, formal, light.

I'm not doing it deliberately when I'm putting a book together, but there's some kind of process similar to that going on in my head. There's the text of the book, and the subtext of the book—and then that third process, kind of an unconscious subtext to the subtext. Reminds me of an old long-play recording I heard once, Bruno Walter rehearsing the Vienna Philharmonic in a performance of a Mozart symphony, the *Jupiter*. No, the *Linz*, that was the one. *The Birth of a Performance* the recording was called. You heard Bruno Walter taking the orchestra through it bar by bar, movement by movement. Wonderful. But the real magical moments were when the passages began to come out exactly like he wanted them to—and as the sound soared up into the air he kept calling excitedly "Zing out! Zing out!" Now and then I get that same feeling from somebody's words as I'm putting them down in their final version on the page—"Sing out! Sing out!" Great moments—not to be the composer, Mozart, but the conductor, the conduit, Bruno Walter.

Meyer gave me the ability to feel all of that, he instilled it into me. I owe him a lot, and not just in him helping me to enjoy music either. He did the same for me in taking me around art galleries, to painting exhibitions and things of that sort. They've been another deep influence in the pleasure they've brought, and in the way I look at things. The mind's eye, the painter's eye, the writer's eye: I don't think you can separate them.

I'm going over some of the ground that's to do with the editing of the material, but that doesn't matter. Because editing is the part that matters, it's that that makes the difference between whether the reader's going to want to go on with the book or not. If he does, great: if he doesn't, for all the good and original material you've got, you could just as well throw your stuff in the trash can.

.   .   .

—The death penalty, yeah, let's talk about that. It's something I've been absolutely opposed to as long as I can remember. Meyer again, something else I got from him. He pointed out that all it was was revenge. Any talk about it being a deterrent is crap. There's not one state in America where they've reintroduced the death penalty after a period of abolition, where the murder rate's gone down as a result, not one. And there's not one country in the world where when they've abolished it and as a result the murder rate's gone up, not one.

Why don't those who are for it be honest about it and say that it is revenge they want, plain and simple, instead of trying to disguise it? OK so I suppose we've got to accept there are basic things like revenge that human beings want, but why don't we have the honesty to say that instead of pretending about it? But we don't give free rein to all our basic instincts, so why do we allow this one to go unchecked? Anyhow, what kind of a society do we live in where we tell people it's OK to kill other people in certain circumstances—like in war, when you can go ahead and kill as many of the enemy as you like: men, women, children, young and old—and get medals for it—but you mustn't do it for personal reasons, like hating someone because he's done you some harm?

Who's crazy about this? I guess I am, if the public-opinion polls are anything to go by. The other day I read eight out of ten people in the States would support the reintroduction of capital punishment nationwide tomorrow. Eight out of ten! When I was younger it used to be in the region of an equal split, fifty for, fifty against, I think it was something like that. I don't know how they measure these things, but if this new figure's right and eight out of ten are for it now, then we're sliding back into barbarism aren't we?

No, I've never changed my mind about the death penalty. I told you about the school debate and the way that teacher made me argue *for* it, which I did. But it was never more than a mental exercise. Alongside of it too of course was my admiration for Clarence Darrow, that was one of the reasons I identified with him, because he was opposed to it. "The advocate for the damned" they called him, when he saved Leopold and Loeb from the electric chair,

But things don't seem to change much either, people's attitudes I mean. Someone I interviewed in *Division Street* told me she knew someone who worked as a secretary in the warden's office in a county jail, and every time a date was announced for an execution in the electric chair of someone who was on death row there, they had a flood of phone calls from people asking could they have tickets to come and watch? She compared it to the same instinct as the one which drove spectators to the Colosseum in Rome.

When I'm challenged to suggest suitable alternatives to it and asked if I don't think we have a right to punish, as well as protect ourselves from dangerous killers, I say yes we do have a right in both cases. The alternative is life imprisonment, if necessary for a long period, up to and including life. This provides protection, and it also if it's reconsidered at intervals, allows for the possibility of reform or redemption or whatever name you like to give it. Putting the death penalty into effect doesn't— and it doesn't allow you any chance of correcting your mistake if you happen to have got the wrong guy, which isn't unknown. I guess we really should have a long careful think about capital punishment. Other countries can do without it. Are we saying we're so barbaric we can't?

The one biggest change that has taken place in attitudes I do have is in the way I look at war. When they dropped the atom bombs on Hiroshima and Nagasaki, like the rest of us I thought "That's the end of the war, we've won, oh great." That would be what, fifty years ago, 1945? Over that period of time my stance has changed a lot. I guess I couldn't call myself an out-and-out pacifist, I'm too aggressively natured for that, but one thing's sure and that's that I'm antiwar. By anybody, for any reason. The person who had the biggest influence on me about it was James Cameron, who I met in 1966 when he was not long back from Vietnam. He'd long before that time had the sense to see that with the weapons human beings had invented and were going on developing, in international affairs if you went down the road to war you were going to come to a dead end. That was his phrase, by the way, and it was a good one and a true one.

He was one of the earliest supporters in your country of what was called CND, the Campaign for Nuclear Disarmament. It began around 1960 right? There were demonstrations and marches in London and to a place called Aldermaston which was an atomic research establishment. Bertrand Russell was connected with it too, and another guy, Canon Collins. They all saw the way things were going, and Cameron used to talk a lot in that calm persuasive way he had that made you stop and think, or maybe I should say stop and rethink. It's not a thing that comes easy if you're an American—the usual course of action is more often to do something and then think about it afterwards, or do it and promise yourself you *will* think about it afterwards, but somehow you never get around to it.

I'm generalizing here I guess, but it's hard to turn yourself around. I mean for a guy in his fifties, like I was when I met Cameron, to have to say to himself "What have I been thinking all these years? Is it time I'd better start over?" Well, that's some achievement on Cameron's part that he could make just one person feel that way. I'm not saying he took all my ideas and stood them on their heads. But he was a profound influence, and just coming into contact with a guy like him changes you in ways you may not be aware of at the time but they stay with you. That's how it was for me.

I never knew what made him the way he was. It always seemed to me he was a natural-born radical: you get the feeling he'd always been that way, it wasn't something he'd adopted because it was fashionable to be like that. Not like they call "radical chic," you know what I mean? "Radical chic"—my God, that's a phrase that makes me wince! You don't ever hear of "conservative chic" do you, or "indifferent chic"? It's a put-down phrase now too, "radical chic" isn't it, yeah you're right.

There's lots of things since I'd like to have talked with him about and heard his views on. When I was working on the book *Race* there were times I would have tried out an idea or two on him, to see what his reaction was. He had a stance, he had a point of view, but he had detachment as well: he could stand back from a thing and look at it dispassionately even though he felt passionately, you know what I mean? There were some things didn't come out in that book—or well, maybe they were touched on but not highlighted enough. He would have been able to point me in the direction of where I could find material to give some more weight to them. I'm thinking of something like the European historical background to the slave trade. A lot of the slave traders who brought African Negroes to America were British, through ports like Liverpool and Bristol, isn't that right? It would have been valuable to get a British perspective on that through the eyes of someone like James Cameron. He would have seen the picture in the round—been appalled by and condemned the traders of course, but discussed as well what sort of people they were and whether they could have been different and behaved any differently. I think there was no way they could have: their whole background and education and upbringing conditioned them to think of black people as inanimate things, like blocks of wood or bales of cotton—objects that were traded in. That isn't to excuse what they did, but maybe it goes a way towards explaining how they could do it. That's the sort of idea I'd like to have heard Cameron say what he thought about it—from the other end of the spectrum, the senders' end rather than what we hear here, which is the receivers' end.

They couldn't think of black people as *people* . . . which, what was it—oh yeah, I know, it reminds me of something else I meant to tell you about but forgot, that time we were talking about celebrities. Like Michael Jordan—he's black, but he's a big celebrity so we don't think of him as black. And Oprah Winfrey—do you have her talk show syndicated over on your television? Did you see the one she had last year about the color problem? Oh boy, there was a moment in that one you wouldn't believe! Well she's black and she's a big celebrity, and on this particular show she's walking around with her mike in her hand among the audience like she usually does—and she stops by different people to ask them to give their opinion—in this instance, about what can be done to increase racial harmony between blacks and whites. Everybody in the audience of course is hoping they'll be one of the ones she picks on, and they'll be seen talking on television with the famous Oprah Winfrey. And she stops by one little old white guy, as close as you and me are now, and she asks him. The moment he opens his mouth you can tell from his accent he's from the South—and this guy, he's a completely crazy racist! "Oprah" he says to her, "I'm telling you, and I'm telling you now"—and he's saying it in warm friendly tones like a man might use to his own daughter—"I'm telling you now, nothing can be done. Because you see, Oprah" he says, "all niggers are dumb—and crazy—and stupid—and they don't have any brains in their heads at all!" And she's there, and she's listening to him, and nodding her head, and encouraging him to go on and on—which he does. It's "Oprah, all niggers are this" and "Oprah, all niggers are that"—and there she is, right there in front of him, and this is his great moment in life, talking on television to the famous Oprah Winfrey, and she's a celebrity, and he doesn't see her as black at all! If there's ever a museum of television history, that one should be in a place of honor all on its own.

Do I think it'll ever change? Some days yes some days no is the answer to that one. Everything, our society, our age . . . I feel optimistic some days, pessimistic others. How does the opening of A Tale of Two Cities go? "It was the best of times, it was the worst of times, it was the age of wisdom, it was the age of foolishness, it was the epoch of belief, it was the epoch of incredulity, it was the season of light, it was the season of darkness, it was the spring of hope, it was the winter of despair." That's how I feel. A great guy your Charles Dickens, he summed it up there pretty well.

The best time of all so far? Well I'd say the 1960s. That was a great time, thirty years ago, that decade. Right now, it's fashionable to decry them, but I don't go along with it. It was a time when young people expressed themselves, they used their imagination, they started in on making what looked like it was going to be a whole new way of life. I know there was our involvement in Vietnam—but there was a positive ending to that, because for the first time I know of, public opinion became so strongly against a war that the government finally had to listen to it and withdraw our troops. And yeah, there was a lot of experimenting went on in drug taking, but mostly because it was the in thing to do. The way I see it, it didn't have any serious or long-lasting deleterious effects.

Young people today, they seem to have lost so much of their imagination somehow. And the benefits of the sixties outweighed the drawbacks didn't they, especially in the field of music. A decade that could throw up a phenomenon like the Beatles, that was really something wasn't it? My all-time favorite of theirs was the one, I don't know its title, but its first line is "You say goodbye and I say hello." Don't ask me why, it just gets to me somehow, it expresses—well, I don't know what: if I did, maybe it wouldn't be as meaningful for me, would it? It expresses the inexpressible, how about that, is that a good enough reason? It's what it leaves to your imagination isn't it? "I say hello"—to what? That's the open-ended fascination part of it.

Where've we gone? From the death penalty to the Beatles, taking in Dickens on the way—that's not bad. Some of the castellations on the castles of the mind.

12

American Friends (2)

Sydney Lewis, Writer

Vernon Jarrett, Television Presenter

Calvin Trillin, *New Yorker* Staff Writer

André Schiffrin, Publisher

Dr. Quentin Young, Internist

Sydney Lewis, Writer

Her first book, Hospital: An Oral History of Chicago's Cook County Hospital, *had just been published.*

"Meet me on Thursday afternoon at WFMT" she wrote. "I was Studs' assistant for eight years, and I'll be delighted to speak with you about him. I love him dearly, tease him mercilessly, and admire him greatly."

—After I left college I worked for a senator, then I was on an Oregon newspaper a while, then I did some bartending, then one day a friend from college days told me there was a secretarial opening here where we're talking at WFMT, and they took me on as a floater. That seems to be standard procedure. You move around from one department to another, wherever they need you.

Most of my time I was a program department assistant, and Norman Pellegrini was my boss. I was around Studs a lot, and you know what he's like, he's the same with everyone—you're good friends, on first-name terms after a couple of days. He's always "Studs" to everyone. I don't know anyone who calls him "Mr. Terkel" longer than ten minutes after they've first met. And he always used to call me "kid." His standard greeting, it was always the same: "Hi kid, what do you hear, what do you say?"

He was very much a one-man band, he didn't have his own personal assistant or secretary. So I made myself one to him, and after a while I worked a lot for him. Rather I should say *with* him, because that's how he made you feel. Life was hectic, he's like a whirlwind: but we got along pretty good. Maybe it's because we've got a fundamental thing in common—we're both New Yorkers by birth and Chicagoans by adoption and where we've spent most of our lives, so that gives us good rapport.

I don't mean by that though our relationship was always harmonious, because it wasn't. Oh no! We'd scream and shout at each other plenty— well, I'd scream and shout, he never did, he just did the things that made me do it. I mean he's like a child, you know—if he wants something he's got to have it *now*. He'd suddenly ask me to find him some recording and he had to have it immediately, so he'd go on about it until I'd bawl at him he'd have to wait till I'd finished doing letters he'd asked me to type urgently an hour before—that sort of thing. Everyone else in the office would think it was very funny to hear me raging at him that way, and he'd look mystified about it. He doesn't bear grudges but I do, and when I'd calmed down I'd be all cool and distant with him for an hour or two until I felt he'd been paid back for his bad behavior . . . did I say *he* was childish?

Anyhow, you get the general picture. But those eight years I spent here with him were the best years of my life so far. I learned so much from him—about books, about people, about working with people—and he was always so supportive to me in my own efforts at writing, too. He'd read something I'd show him that I'd written, and he'd say "Heh kid, you wrote this? This is good!"

And he was always so caring about everybody he worked with, you know? After I'd been here a couple of years I went on vacation to my dad's in Massachusetts, and I'd no sooner got there than I went down with a bad MS attack and had to go into the hospital. When I came out the doctors told me to stay off work and rest for six whole weeks, and Studs called me there on the phone every single day. He'd say "Are they going to fix it, kid, they can fix it can't they?" The first day I came back into work here, there were a dozen roses on my desk.

My own book *Hospital* is done in the same way that Studs does his because it never occurred to me to do it any other way. The form was one I was happy using—and the idea for the book itself, like so many of Studs's, came from André Schiffrin. I knew him because of his frequent contacts with Studs and visits to him, and he said to me one day he thought somebody should try and give a picture of a big hospital by interviewing a cross section of its people. I said I thought that was a great idea, and André said "Well how about you doing it?" That hadn't entered my head, and I was very nervous about it as you can guess. I was surprised to get the hospital's agreement, but when I did I went ahead and did a couple of interviews, and then sent them to André and he liked them, so that was how it began.

Of course I've had a certain amount of imprinting from being so close with Studs, and I hope what I've learned from him has been put to good use. He has big ears and big eyes, and I've learned how important those are. In my time with him I've done some transcribing for him: for my own book I did my own, and again, doing that taught me what I think's the most important thing of all, which is to have respect for the person you're interviewing, by knowing when to stop questioning and when to back off if you're trespassing into painful areas of personal feeling. I'm a kind of a nosey broad myself, but I'm learning how to keep myself in check and not let my curiosity run away with me just for the sake of it. And one other thing I've learned is exactly why Studs was always in such a bad mood when he was in the editing phase of one of his own books. Having gone through that phase now myself, I sure can understand how terrible you feel for weeks or months on end while you're doing it.

Everybody knows him as a great writer, with a photographic memory and a photographic ear. I'd like to add as a very personal note that although I'm too young to have known him during the McCarthy era when he was blacklisted and couldn't get work, I know from other people who knew him then how much they admired his principled stance in refusing to give names of anyone to the investigating committee. And I'm saying I know he's still that selfsame principled man. When André Schiffrin left Pantheon, where he was an editor, because of a policy disagreement, Studs was about to finish his book *Race*. He held it back, and waited until André found a way to set up independently as a publisher himself, and then he gave *Race* to him to publish.

I was there when somebody told Studs they'd heard about this, and they thought it was very noble of him to be so loyal to André. And you know, Studs looked at him in genuine amazement. "Noble?" he said. "What's the big deal? How could I possibly do anything else but stay with him? That man gave me my career."

There's no way he's changed.

Vernon Jarrett, Television Presenter

—Where I was born in Paris, Tennessee, all blacks were either labor-ers or house servants, and they had to Uncle Tom—that's give the im-pression they agreed with and were happy being like that—every day of their lives. Both my father and mother were the children of slaves origi-nally, but had had a little education and become schoolteachers. They saw to it that their children had a little education too. And then I came as a young man to Chicago hoping to be a journalist, and I was fortunate enough to find employment with the black newspaper called *The De-fender.*

I don't exactly remember what the circumstances were that first brought me into contact with Studs. One thing I know for sure is that he will, with that colossal memory of his. I'll recall an instance of that for you later on if you'll remind me. I should imagine it was a civil rights meeting or something of that kind, because we were both very much involved in the movement. As much or more than anyone else I know, he's been for equality of treatment for blacks. In fact, I can't think of any other white person I've ever met in my life who knows so much about black history—by which I mean black feeling and black life.

I was aware of that quality in him from almost the very beginning of what's now been almost a forty-year friendship. It's true what I once heard somebody say, that being black in a predominantly white-populated area in any city in America you care to name, is like wearing an ill-fitting pair of shoes—you look all right in them to everyone else, and you know yourself you do—but it's only you who knows the discom-fort you're in when you start to move around.

Well, I think—no, I know—I can say that Studs hasn't got that feeling in him towards me or any other black person. Nor has his lovely wife Ida—they're a wonderful little couple. And the one particularly special thing about him is that it's not an intellectual white liberal feeling of sympathy towards you that they have—it's an identification that's so total and so natural that they don't notice it and neither do you. And there's no pretense in him about it, no gamesmanship. I could take Studs into a meeting or a church service where the audience or congregation would be entirely black, where he'd be the one single white person there. And how it would come about I don't know, but no one would look at him twice nor would he look at anyone there twice. He just would not be or seem to be intrusive or obtrusive, or in any way noticeable or out of place at all.

I have cherished knowing him all my life, and it seems to me he's always been in it all the time. In the good times and the bad, Studs has been my friend. In the good times of my successes, Studs has been my friend. In the down times, the bad times, the sad times like when my son died last year, Studs has been at my side. I would trust him with my thoughts and feelings as I'd trust no one else, whether they be black or white. I admire the insight which he brings to bear, particularly on black issues of course, but I'm not talking specifically about those. They're the same that he has for everything and for everyone. Simply put, I'd say he was a very genuine human being, and I think this is because he treats everyone he meets as though they were a celebrity. I've been with him many times when he'll start a conversation with a cabdriver, or someone standing next to him waiting to cross the street at a light, and in ten seconds he's deep in conversation with them about some world issue or other, it's quite amazing.

I used to think it was a special skill he had, this ability to get people to talk, and I've in the past tried to study it and learn how to do it, when I've heard him interviewing people or been interviewed by him myself. My idea of course was to try and copy it if I could sometimes with a guest on my own TV show. But a long time ago I came to the conclusion that no, it's not a skill he's got: it's a gift, a natural gift.

A wonderful example of it, which I know and you could say was from an insider's point of view, is his interview with me in his book *American Dreams: Lost and Found*. It's me talking about my childhood, and it takes up twelve printed pages. It appears to be a monologue, apart from a single question of his own in the middle which he's left in. Now let me tell you that didn't take place under any prearranged or formal interlocutor-interviewee situation at all. We just happened to run into each other on the street one day, and exchanged a few this-and-thats, and he told me about this book he was doing. And without knowing I was doing it, I started to tell him myself about where and how I grew up. I think he said something like "If you've the time, while you're talking let's go back to my office"—and without making an attempt to conceal it, he took his tape recorder out of his pocket and switched it on as we walked along, with me still talking. And I went on talking and talking as one memory followed another, and he would throw in a question every once in a while, prompting. It was all so easy to do, and how long I talked for I've no idea.

In the book it's a long piece, but on tape it must have been much longer of course. But the technique was that there was no technique, he was a friend listening with genuine interest to what I was telling him. That's an example of what I mean when I say it's not something I could study and learn and put into practice, it's not as simple as that.

Yes and his colossal memory facility I spoke of earlier, I do recall a good example of that that happened just the other day. He'd called me up about something, and he asked me how my wife was. Her name's Fernetta by the way, but she always gets to be called "Fern." And Studs said "And how's your beautiful wife, how's Fern?" So I said oh she was good thank you, and then he said "Now you take good care of her, you've got a very beautiful lady there—do you remember that first time you brought her to meet me and Ida, and she wore that beautiful blue dress and how lovely she looked, and we had dinner at the Triangle Restaurant upstairs there?" I'm saying "Oh. Yeah. Yeah Studs. Yeah, that's right." And even *I* don't remember what color her dress was— because the time he's talking about when I took her to meet them was over forty years ago!

Calvin Trillin, *New Yorker* staff writer

We talked while we drank coffee in the modernly furnished and spacious open-plan living area on the second floor of his house in Greenwich Village, New York. A relaxed and friendly man, with the soft traces of a Kansas origin still in his voice.

—I first met Studs when he interviewed me on his radio show in Chicago, when I was doing a book-promotion tour to coincide with the publication of my first or second comic novel, I don't remember which. You get so used to being asked the same questions and answering them with the same answers when you do those tours—"Mr. Trillin, what gave you the idea for doing this book? Well for a time when I left college I worked for a small-town newspaper. Oh, so are your characters based on real people you worked with then? No, not on real characters, but on a sort of synthesis of several of them put together. And the incidents, like when the mayor's wife feels around in the closet for her leather belt and pulls out the boa constrictor that's hanging down in there—did that really happen? Oh no I made that up entirely." And it goes on, and the next place you're at, out come the same questions and your selfsame answers, and before long you start thinking to yourself "What the hell am I doing here, this is purgatory, did I ever really write such a stupid book as this one we're talking about?"

And then I get to Chicago, and I go in the studio with Studs and he produces his copy with all his underlinings and scrawls on it of questions he wants to ask about it. He's obviously read it very perceptively, and he quotes passages from it, and he gets you to read out parts of it—and in no time at all you're thinking "Heh, this is interesting, actually it's not as bad as I thought it was, it's not bad at all." In fact ever since I had that experience, I've often thought of suggesting to publishers that if they've got an author whose morale's getting a bit low, they should send him or her to Chicago to be interviewed by Studs Terkel to lift their spirits again.

Then of course after the interview he takes you out to lunch, and that in itself is another whole new experience. Whenever I'm in Chicago now, we go out, and even though he's a celebrity there, it's still just like going out with an ordinary guy and meeting a lot of his friends. At the restaurant where you're eating people are all the time coming up to the table and asking him how he is, and the waiters and cooks come out of the kitchen and do the same. I remember last year we took a cab to go some place to eat, and the driver and Studs obviously knew each other. This guy was a Nigerian, and Studs immediately started asking him had he been back there since he'd seen him before. He knew exactly what part of Nigeria he came from, and he asked him for an update on farming conditions there, on his family, everything. In a city with a population of three million, Studs must know two million nine hundred and ninety-nine thousand nine hundred and ninety-nine, and the only reason he doesn't know the other one is they've never happened to ride the same bus together. Have some more coffee? Help yourself.

In the old days when you went to Chicago, if you were from out of town they took you to visit the stockyards. Nowadays they take you to introduce you to Studs Terkel. He's their icon, and though I haven't seen

him a couple of years now, I know if we happened to pass on Fifth
Avenue here, he'd recognize me immediately and start asking me for an
update on what I was doing, how my wife Alice was, what our children
were doing. And that's not just because we worked together a few years
back doing TV and radio shows in California and here in New York, it's
because he's like that with everybody.

The radio program I enjoyed doing most with him was based on a
newspaper column I used to do. It was "Daddy-Daughter Breakfast Conversations," we recorded some and they were broadcast. I was "Daddy"
and Studs was the kid "Daughter" and he played her in that wonderful
nasal twang gangster-hoodlum voice of his. I don't have any of the actual
scripts here right now, but it'd go something along these lines, and you
have to imagine Studs's voice for it:

—Can I have some more cereal please Daddy?
—Sure honey, go right ahead, help yourself.
—Daddy, I see in that newspaper you're reading that the taxes on
  gasoline are going to be upped again.
—Oh really? Oh yes, so it does say that, that's right honey.
—Daddy, didn't the president promise in his reelection campaign
  that if he served a second term, he'd cut all the taxes?
—Er yeah, yeah I believe he did honey.
—Does that mean the president doesn't always tell the truth,
  Daddy?

Not all of them would be as overtly political as that, but we got a lot of
fun doing them. Like so many of these things, we always had more ideas
for targets than we could ever use.

Our television shows, they were half-hour chat shows on a wide range
of different subjects. We had one on jazz of course, one on street enter-
tainers, another on architects, another on photography, one on operatic
divas and so on. We co-hosted and co-interviewed, all very relaxed and
informal. It gave me an opportunity to watch him at work. I never failed
to be amazed at some of the things he did. For a moment there I was
going to say "the stunts he pulled"—but they weren't stunts, they were
things he did naturally and spontaneously, and they worked wonderfully
well because they were so original.

One instance in particular I remember was one night he was interviewing somebody, and as usual he was putting the whole of himself into the conversation. You know, being very genuinely as always deeply interested in the subject they were discussing. As the allotted time for the program end came near, the director as usual off camera gave the signal to Studs to start on the windup. The usual thing is the interviewer says words like "Well I'm afraid that's all we've got time for" or something to that effect. Professional that he is, Studs caught the director's signal out of the corner of his eye: so, in a very brief pause he turned full-face to camera and said "Good night," and then turned back to the person he was talking to and carried on with the conversation as the credits rolled. It was astonishing. I've seen him do it a time or two since, and he never rehearses it, but he always seems to know when it'll be effective.

Another of his techniques—I think all interviewers should do it—is he never tries to demonstrate how smart he is, never catches someone out with a question. His radio show succeeds through his guests, he doesn't want to top them. It's their show, not *The Studs Terkel Show*.

Oh and a final thought—something that's always struck me is how evocative of Chicago the name "Studs" is. It fits him like a glove. You couldn't imagine him being called "Bud" Terkel or "Richard" Terkel, or "William Jones"—William Jones'd probably be a bank manager, or so you'd imagine. With a name like that he could even be a Republican folksinger if it was possible for there to be such a thing. "Studs Terkel" resonates with Chicago, doesn't it?

André Schiffrin, Publisher

Among the acknowledgments at the beginning of Coming of Age *is "a bow to my publisher and editor, André Schiffrin, who has always been there"—and the comprehensiveness of it is justified by the fact that he is credited with being the idea originator of eight of Studs Terkel's books (the two exceptions being* Giants of Jazz *which was written before they met, and* Chicago *which was produced at the invitation of someone else, as a text to accompany photographs.) The partnership—which is what both describe it as—has been a remarkably productive one, coming as it does from a mental affinity between two men who, superficially at least, seem totally unlike each other.*

Whereas Studs is spirited and outgoing, the quiet spoken André Schiffrin is somewhat distancing and austere in manner, occasionally sharp in tone, and appears cautious in revealing his feelings. More like, one could almost say, an Englishman than an American.

We talked in his office in his publishing house, The New Press, in New York.

—I'd spent two years at Cambridge reading history at the same time as Eleanor Bron was there, and I came into publishing afterwards (my father was a publisher). When Eleanor was here touring with *The Establishment* she met Studs in Chicago—I expect you know all this—and then when she came on to New York she suggested I should meet him. I'd already read some of his interviews that had been published in the WFMT magazine, and I'd also heard some of his network broadcasts, so I was familiar with his work.

At that time I was with Random House, at Pantheon Books, where we'd published a book of interviews called *Report from a Chinese Village* which had done quite well, and I was thinking of doing a series of roughly parallel books from different countries. So I called up Studs and asked him what did he think of doing one on an American village, only in this case making the village his city, Chicago. After some thought he seemed to like the idea, and agreed to go ahead and do it. That was its origin, the genesis of it in my mind—as a book that would be one of a series about different places by different authors. I didn't envisage *Division Street* as having the reception that it did. It made him famous, rightly, as an oral historian, and was a tremendous success in its own right, which of course I'm very happy about. Since I left Pantheon and set up here, I've started to reissue some of his books, and that and *Talking to Myself* are the ones I've begun with and have already published new editions of.

Studs has always been very generous in acknowledging my ideas for him to work on, and their being the mainspring of his books. I suppose there's some truth in it, in that I do prompt him with ideas, and in that sense we have a partnership. But my contribution is very limited, of course, compared with the amount of work actually involved in producing the book itself, which is his: I don't have a hand in it again until the editorial stage.

There are very many authors, the majority I should think, who prefer their own ideas to those coming from other people. Some of them I'd never even think of making a suggestion to, so Studs is unusual in being very open to working in that way. But I do put up ideas to him, too, that don't tempt him and he doesn't proceed with: or sometimes he'll think something might work but after he's started find it isn't going to work out. A year or two back we thought we might try and do a book on power but we never got off first base on that. When Studs started to talk to some of the big corporate bosses, they all denied they had any real power, and the idea was one we had to abandon. Another one that fell by the wayside was one about young people: he started, turned the subject around in his mind and spoke to a few people—but he was never at ease with it, so we gave up on that one too. Instead we eventually went to the opposite end of the spectrum and did *Coming of Age* about old people.

The way I help with the editing is chiefly with the cutting down of the material he gets. Not so much shortening the individual contributions as deciding who to take out and who to leave in, which is very tricky. He becomes so involved himself with the people he's talked to, that it's useful for him to have an outsider's view of who's more effective and germane to his theme, and who's less so. We kept only about one word in ten, on the first book: he brought in somewhere around a million words and we reduced it to a hundred thousand. We never alter anybody's phrasing, we sometimes reorder a little, and we always try to keep the rhythm of the way a person speaks.

All writers have their neuroses of course, and his particular one, which never seems to lessen, is about whether he can really write or not—or is he just a purveyor of other people's words? He's always asking me this question, and I suppose himself and everyone else—"Can I write?" It's hard to understand that he can mean to be taken seriously, because of course *Talking to Myself* demonstrates vividly that he can—and this introduction he's written to his new book *Coming of Age* I think is one of the most eloquent things he's ever done.

His output, his whole work over the last twenty-five years, has been remarkable in its consistently high standard, and shows no sign of flagging. Not all his books have had the same amount of success—that's because different works have appealed to different people. I think *Working* and *"The Good War"* have been the two biggest sellers because of the universality of their subject appeal. The least popular in terms of sales, probably because they were more challenging and critical of popular attitudes, were *Race* and *The Great Divide.* Those two undoubtedly made many feel uncomfortable, because it's been said quite truly I think that in them people tell the truth about what they're thinking and feeling, even when they're lying to themselves. To get them to do that's one of his many great gifts of course.

I'd say the thing I've most admired him for as a man, is how he survived that dreadful time of the McCarthy witch-hunting here, when he was blacklisted and couldn't get work. He was very severely marginalized, and no one who didn't undergo the experience can ever really know what it must have been like. The *Chicago Tribune* for example wouldn't even list his radio program in their daily listings, and treated it as though it didn't exist, and him as though he was a nonperson.

But survive he did, and work, and build up the reputation worldwide for himself which he has now. Some people still don't like him of course—he doesn't by any means charm all the savage beasts in this jungle of ours. Young and old ultra-right-wing reviewers still occasionally are dismissive, disrespectful and downright unpleasant about his work, being very nasty on purely political grounds and accusing him of playing the same old left-wing popular-front melodies on and on and on. How you can say that about someone who purveys the words of people of all creeds and ages and races, and both the privileged and the deprived, I don't know. But that's what he's done and what he'll always do, I do know that.

Dr. Quentin Young, Internist

A lively mannered and humorous man of seventy, he was formerly director of medicine at Cook County Hospital, Chicago, and is now in practice in the Hyde Park area of the city with three younger partners. His practice of medicine is that of a general internist.

—In this country it means you're a physician, not a surgeon: Your speciality is general medical treatment for adults. I like it, I've always practiced it. Surgeons I think are at their happiest when their patients are asleep, but for me the give-and-take relationship with another person is much more enjoyable. Sharing my knowledge and explaining a treatment I'm giving, and why, is becoming increasingly popular, and I think it should be. You'll still come across the occasional patient who doesn't want to know about things and whose attitude is that you're some kind of miracle worker: and there may be the odd old-fashioned arrogant doctor who likes to be thought of that way. But those attitudes are dying out, thankfully. I think a lot of it's due to media provision of information which is very responsible, mostly.

Our practice is in the same area where Studs lives, which is how I come to be his doctor, which I have been for very many years. He says we first met a long time before he and Ida came to live there, but I've no recollection of it myself. I mean I do vaguely remember the incident he describes, and knowing what his memory is, I'm sure he's probably right about the fact we did have a conversation. But the time he says it occurred was when I was twelve years old! It was when he was a radio actor in a soap opera, and I went along and auditioned for a small part there was in one or two episodes for a kid. He describes what I was wearing and what we had our casual chat together about, all in great detail—and as I say, he's probably right. But how in hell he could remember it all when we didn't meet again till forty years later, when he arrived at our practice one day, don't ask me!

For a man of his age, he's in a wonderful state of health, which is because he's sensible and looks after himself. Or maybe I should say that Ida sees to it he looks after himself. She takes great care of him, there's no doubt about that. He's moderate in what he does; he drinks a little, he used to smoke cigars but he's given that up, and he calls me up slightly more often than he needs to and says "Hi Quent, isn't it about time I had another checkup?"

But he's not hypochondriacal about it, he doesn't overuse my services. He wouldn't take advantage of our friendship to get me to give him more time than I would any other patient, or do him any special favors. He takes his turn in the waiting room along with everyone else, which surprises some of the other patients, who see him and recognize him and think he's sure to get preferential treatment. It's not offered, he doesn't expect it, and I know he wouldn't accept it if it were.

We're close personal friends and meet often. One disease we have in common is that of talking too much, which afflicts us both as soon as we come into contact. He'll come to see me by appointment at the practice because he's having a slight pain in his chest or something, and as soon as he comes through the door into my room he starts in on something about medical ethics he's read of in the paper that day. Let's say for example, it's some doctors protesting having to be present at executions by lethal injection, and I start telling him I'm going to try and organize a medical group to take a stand against it in Illinois. In one minute flat we're both expressing our mutual indignation, and I say "Well anyway tell me some more about this chest pain you're having." And he says "That can wait, we'll get round to that later, I've just thought of who might be able to advise us on the best way to get this group going." And by the time we *do* get round to his chest pain and I've examined him, he's probably decided it wasn't bad enough for him to have troubled me about it.

We both have this diversionary and irrelevant affliction and recognize it. He says I'm worse than he is, but I don't think so. And I know there are days when a good doctor-patient conversation is much better therapy than any kind of drug prescribing—I know it because I've more than once experienced it myself: on a day when I may not have been feeling too good, after he's been to see me I've felt much better.

It's difficult to think of anything critical to say about him—and I'm not saying that out of loyalty to a friend, but because he affects everyone the same way. He's exceptionally gregarious, and wherever he goes he's always the same—amiable and affable, switching from joking to seriousness and then back to being amusing again, all the time. I've never known him to be rude to anyone, or unkind to anyone, even though they may have been so to him. It doesn't seem to be in his nature to be retaliatory at all. And yet despite that you could never consider him to be pious or saintly or unctuous or anything of that kind, because you can't be anything else but at ease in his presence.

I did meet one person—and it's only one, in the whole of the past twenty years—who the first time he met him said to me afterwards he thought Studs was a bit of a phony, and he found his kind of perpetual "on stage" personality off-putting. I remembered his phrase about it because I'd never heard anyone else ever say it: he said he wished Studs would behave "more naturally." Well it just so happened this person came into contact with him several more times over the next few years, and one night after I'd seen them cozying up together and having a good laugh about something at a drinks party, I said to him, "Oh you seem to get on OK with Studs now do you?" He gave me a puzzled look and he said "Why, what do you mean? Didn't I ever?" I reminded him he'd once told me he wished he'd behave "more naturally"—and he was astounded, he said "I never said that, I've never met a more natural behaved guy in my life!"

So there you have it. Is that a criticism of Studs? I bet you'll never do better.

13

You Say Goodbye and I Say Hello: Studs Talking (4)

—How would you like we should wind it all up in our last interviews between us? You got enough material to make some kind of sense of it?

What have *I* got out of it—apart from the pleasure of talking so much about myself, you mean? Huh, maybe I should add not always all that much of a pleasure either, which is how it should be, I guess.

OK, what have I got out of it? Well I'll try and tell you. First off, there's a funny thing I didn't expect which is talking so much about my mother, and thinking about her in between, I feel I've come to understand her a little better. I think she was in a kind of a strange way—I hope this doesn't sound patronizing of feminists—I think of her own times, you know, she was a sort of a feminist. An individual, a person in her own right, in days when women were only supposed to be submissive and inferior to men. She didn't have a lot of education, she worked hard all her life to support an ailing husband and bring up her children: but when she got the chance to run hotels, she applied herself to learning and applying business principles so as to make a success of it. Which she did, and paid back my uncle the money he'd put up for us to get started. She didn't have too good a personality, so she couldn't make her way by using feminine charm and wiles or anything of that sort. And she got no thanks or regard for it: quite the contrary, most people disliked her and were scared of her. I reckon she was shortchanged on the give-and-take of life's pleasantries.

So I guess that's been the number-one benefit to me that's come out of this. Number two—well, it's not a benefit, because I wouldn't have

expected anything different from you—but it's an expression of grati-
tude that you've kept your word, and you've not harassed me or pursued
me into areas that you knew were painful and I didn't want to talk about.
I'm flawed, of course, who isn't? Life's not been a bed of roses all the
way, not for me nor for Ida, nor for my son and my relationship with
him. But whether they want to talk to you, or will talk to you, is entirely
for them to decide and not something I'll try in any way to influence
them about.

But the flaws in what might be called not my private but my public
life—sure, I'll talk to you about those if you like, why not? I guess they'll
make up a whole extra book-length work on their own if you've got the
patience for it.

No, I don't remember the first question I ever asked you about myself
when you said you were going to try and do this book, what was it? "Do I
use people?" Oh was that what it was, "Do I use people?" Well of course
the answer's yes. Yes of course I do, I use people all the time, there's no
getting away from it. And sometimes I don't think I'm too kind about it
either. It's something that's in my nature. I recognize it as a fault, and
one that can be unpleasant. But it's deeply ingrained in me now. I don't
suppose I'll ever be rid of it. I'll give you an example.

In one of my books I have an interview with a social worker, or an ex–
social worker I should say, about the sort of humiliation some of the
poor and underprivileged had to undergo. My wife Ida used to be a
social worker, so I asked her if she'd ever experienced such a situation.
She said yes she had, so I went and got out my tape recorder, and turned
it on and asked her to tell me about it. It had happened a few years
before, she said, and she told me she'd had to go assess the circumstances of an elderly man claiming benefit. He lived in a run-down tene-
ment block, and she said he was very quietly spoken, very dignified in the
way he answered the embarrassing questions about his circumstances she
needed to ask him. Then at the end she said to him "I'm sorry, but I'm
supposed to look in your closet." And he said to her "Please go ahead,
I've nothing to hide"—so she slid back the door and looked in his closet.
And it was totally empty, he had no clothes in it at all. And in telling it,
Ida said "He was so humiliated—and I was too"—and she started crying,
and asked me to switch the tape recorder off. And I said "No, go on, this
is great, go on" and I wouldn't switch it off.

Ida gets furious when I tell people this story. She says I seem to take pride in showing myself up to be so heartless. But you know, it's not that: I'm trying to describe how I am. It's not just the tape recorder I can't switch off, it's me I can't switch off either. There's always some part of me that's outside, detached, observing. Whatever the situation, however emotional in any way it might be, there's a—I don't know, a something sitting right here on my shoulder taking it all in—both the other person and me, and what's going on between us. Only once in my whole life did that not operate: it was the day I told you about, the day after my father had died and I was riding the streetcar and I suddenly burst into tears. That's the one moment when I've ever experienced total loss of control, it's the only one.

I've wondered sometimes if this has anything to do with an inhibition I have. It's over a certain word I can't say, it's the word "love"—I've never been able to say to a person, never that simple thing, "I love you." Never. I can't get it out. I can feel it, sure, I think I can feel it—but I can't *say* it. Don't ask me why. People say it to me, Ida says it to me, but I can't say it back. Isn't that crazy?

I've gone offtrack there, I wanted to try and say some more about that detachment feeling, the feeling of watching myself all the time. I gave you the example of hurting Ida because of it. I'll give you another where it's the same but doesn't hurt anyone, which is when I'm acting the clown.

Yeah, yeah, OK I know, is there any time when I'm not acting the clown? That's a good question. It's a better question in fact than you might think. The answer is I'm not sure if there is such a time or not, not any longer. Who was it, Oscar Wilde was it who said some people wear a mask to cover up the mask underneath? I've been so much a clown figure ever since I can remember, that maybe that's the real me after all. I know I'm an entertainer, and I *like* being an entertainer—a clown figure, a Charlie Chaplin, the little guy at odds with the establishment, who doesn't fit in and doesn't want to fit in. He's always been my idol, or the figure he played has. The tramp-clown, the highest praise you can give something to me is to say it's "Chaplinesque."

I don't take life seriously. Sometimes I don't think I take it seriously enough, other times I think I take it too seriously. But whichever, there's always this this this thing on my shoulder here watching me doing it, saying "Studs, you're a ham, you're doing this for the sake of making people laugh." And that's right, I am. It's a character I've chosen to play, and maybe you're right in what your question was suggesting, that I've been playing it so long it's what I've become, down underneath and through and through. It doesn't mean I don't have principles, left-wing or liberal or whatever you like to call them, and antiwar, and anti-Jim Crow legislation and always have been and so on. But you can get a long way by not putting on too-earnest a front about it: don't take me seriously because I am goddam serious about it, you know how I mean? The one thing I won't clown around about though, the one thing is capital punishment.

I've always been a performer, there's always been that need in me to be one. You remember that was why I gave up on law school, when I realized I wasn't going to be the great Clarence Darrow, the courtroom advocate for the damned? I realized I was only going to be a humdrum malfeaser of torts—heh, I like that phrase, I've only just thought that one up—and where was the limelight in that? I *am* an entertainer, I wanted to be loved by the world, who doesn't? I *want* to be one of the boys—but isn't it time to call a halt? *Can* I call a halt? Do I want to, do I need to? Why should I? Where's the harm? You know that moment in *Waiting for Godot?*, in Samuel Beckett's wonderful play? It's the defining moment of it for me. "One day we'll die. The light gleams an instant, then it's night once more." And then Pozzo jerks the rope for Lucky to lead him off the stage and he shouts "On!" and they exit. "On!" That's how I feel, that's where I'm going—"On!" And I've always felt that. And what does Beckett call the play? "A tragicomedy." Well, that's what life is, isn't it? Yeah.

.   .   .

—What were we talking about last time? Oh yeah, about going on. I'd not say driven on, no, I liked it, I want to be, I liked the feeling, it was like the other feeling I told you about once, in the Beatles song, not knowing what was around the corner, "You say goodbye and I say hello," remember? I've always wanted to go on, I've always been the enthusiastic discoverer.

Except once. There was just the one time in my life I did begin to droop, to flag a little. That was the McCarthy time, when I was blacklisted and couldn't get work. Not so much the not-getting-work side of it, that's something a lot of people experience in their lives. It can happen to anyone—bad luck, ill health, shut downs, redundancy. It happens all the time. But that period brought on a very long and sustained time of self-doubt for me, when it was said I wasn't behaving like a true American should.

People have said to me—they might have said it to you too—they thought the stance I took against the Un-American Activities Committee, refusing to give them names of associates I had—was a brave thing to do. Well, I don't go along with that. I was scared, so I did the only thing I knew how to do, not to show it. Like, as usual, horsing around, playing the clown. They said to me something like "Now's the time for all good Americans to stand up and be counted," so I stood up and said "One." They said "We don't think that's very funny, we're holding a serious investigation here." Another time I was advised the thing to do to avoid being listed, was when they asked me did I sign this petition and that petition that had been organized by this or that proscribed Communist organization—say against antiblack labor laws or something of that sort—I should say I'd been duped into signing it.

Well I wouldn't do that, I just said "Yeah I signed it." When they said but it was a known Communist organization I tried to be clever, I said so what, if the Communists had come out against cancer, did that mean I had to sign up to say I was in favor of cancer? They said they didn't think that was very funny either.

Which it wasn't. But that would have seemed very humiliating, it would have made me look stupid, saying I'd been duped. So that was how it was: it wasn't a case of me being heroic or anything, it was just I was clowning around. My ego taking over again was what it was, wasn't it? I've always described myself as an independent, politically, and that's what I am. I'd be the same, whatever the system, left or right.

So what else is there left we haven't covered? Not much I shouldn't think, would you? Oh yeah that's right, religion, I've not said anything about that have I, no. Well what I'd define myself as is an agnostic, which is what someone once told me is a cowardly atheist: that's OK by me, if that's what it is. My father and mother were both Jewish, but not very devout or orthodox. As far as beliefs went, in fact my father was downright skeptical and I think I've inherited that stance from him. I've tried to be ecumenical: sometimes I like to flatter myself by saying I'm religiously eclectic.

But I've never had any faith, no religious belief, I've never made what Kierkegaard called that "leap in the dark" which you have to make if you're to be a true believer. And yet I guess I do have a belief in some kind of immortality, something inside of everyone, a kind of a common humanity that's passed on. It can be called God or the human spirit or anything else: however you name it, I believe that's there. I like to think something of my father lives on in me, and something of me'll live on in my son. I'm talking entirely masculine terms here aren't I, "father," "son"? That's the conditioning of upbringing, yeah? I ought to be including my mother in it as well, shouldn't I? Well I did say to you one time I thought I'd inherited some of her genes, right? I'm no deep religious thinker about these matters as you'll have noticed. That's because I don't spend too much time thinking about the hereafter, I'm too preoccupied with the here and now. Organized religion and churches I don't go for much, there's too many demagogues around. Here in America it's all mixed in with politics too—"the religious right," that's a phrase that's entered our language now. What a misnomer eh, "the religious right"?

What else, what else? At the front of *Talking to Myself* I gave an acknowledgment "To my memory, a blessing and a curse." You noticed that, you took me up on it one time, you asked me to explain. Is this the place to expand on it? OK then. A blessing because it's been useful—to remember people in places, their names, details of conversations you had with them from way back. It's not something you learn how to, you either have it or you don't. I've been lucky, I've had it to a high degree. But a memory like that's a curse too, because it means I remember things I don't *want* to remember, things I'd sooner forget. Incidents I'm not too proud of, that I'd sooner pretend hadn't happened, I can't wipe them out of my mind. That's the downside of it, that's what goes with having a retentive memory, the price you have to pay for it. Someone'll say "It's all over, Studs, it's years back, I've forgotten about it, honest, whatever it was it doesn't mean nothing to me now, whatever it was that caused that bad feeling between us." But *I* do, I remember. It doesn't mean I bear a grudge. But I wish I *could* forget what it was had caused the upset between us, especially if it had been in some ways my fault. There's so many things in me I'd like to hide from myself. We all do, we all have secrets about ourselves we hide from others. Most people do it so long that that's the way they end up, hiding things from themselves until they've obliterated them. I can't. I wish I could.

Can I write? Oh yeah and that's the big one I haven't answered and never will. Can I write—and why is it so important to me I should convince myself I can? It's the ego thing again, isn't it? The uncertainty of never knowing, in spite of what anyone else says, whether you're any good, whether you've any value or not. That was the soft spot the McCarthy time touched on, that was the root of it, was I really any good, did I have any worth? That's why in all the years since, in all the praise, the accolades, the Pulitzer, all the rest, the doubt's still remained. Underneath the clowning, it's there too isn't it? I'm saying OK I'm not taking myself seriously, so it doesn't matter anyway.

Yeah, and anything else underneath all *that*? Well yes there is, and I'll tell you. What's underneath it is a favorite word of mine—the *irony* of it. What's the irony? That I've become celebrated for celebrating the uncelebrated people of the world, built myself a world reputation for giving voice to the voices of those we never hear. No one's aware of that more than I am, of the irony of it.

Oh and one more thing. A big one. Who am I? I've a hunch the people you've visited with for this book, most of them may have said I'm a great guy. Because that's how they see me. But I hope they've not forgotten I'm an actor—and a pretty good one, I suspect. That role I'm playing—"the great guy"—he may be an invented character. The role's one I've been playing more than eighty years now—which would make it one of the longest runs in the history of the theater.

Put that in, OK?

14

Family

Ida Terkel

Roger Smith

Ida Terkel

Tiny and slight—exactly five feet in height and weighing a little over ninety pounds, she has the figure and gliding grace in her movements of a dancer. Brown haired, elfin faced with large modern styled pink rimmed spectacles, she wore tailored blue jeans, a red sweatshirt and sandals. She smiled shyly while she talked, softly clasping and unclasping her hands between her knees, sitting in the middle of the long sofa, underneath a full-sized reproduction of Brueghel's The Peasant's Wedding *high on the wall above her head. "I'm a very private sort of person" she had once said.*

—Well, I was born in a town in northern Wisconsin, and all together there were eight children in our family. I don't know how my parents managed to bring us all up, but they did—they were really quite remarkable people in a way, they must have been mustn't they?

They came to America from the Ukraine. Both of them were Jewish, and it was a struggle for them: at the time I didn't realize how much of a struggle, and I never will really, I suppose. My mother, who was the talkative one in the family, would talk about her trip here sometimes. My father was already here, and she followed with their four children who'd all been born in the Ukraine—three boys and a girl, my elder sister, who was two years old when they came here. I suppose they traveled steerage class, but I don't know what that was really like. It was probably pretty hard for immigrants in those days. Many of them came looking for a new life. Some of the experiences on that boat ride must have been very traumatic for her, because she remembered all the details, and she'd tell them over and over again.

My father hardly ever talked very much about his journey though. He came to Wisconsin because he had a brother there, a little bit younger than he was, and he started working making a living as a traveling pedlar. He spoke Yiddish of course, and he spoke Russian, and also he spoke Polish. Polish was a very useful language to know, because in that part of the country, in Wisconsin, there were many Ukrainian immigrants but also many Polish immigrants too. So because he could speak their language, they waited until he called on them, and then they bought things from him to save themselves the embarrassment of having to go into what few stores there were in the nearest town, where usually they had difficulty in making their wants and needs understood. So he prospered, he did well.

In time he was able to set up a store himself in town, and to send for my mother and their four children to come and join him. I don't remember exactly which order things occurred in, what came first and what second, but I believe it was about a year after he'd come that he sent for her. Then after they came, they had two more children—another boy, and then me. The store prospered as well. My father was a good businessman.

It was always their intention to have six children, and that was how it stayed for five years, with me as the youngest. Then when I was five years old, I got an infection—I'm not sure of what sort. Of course there weren't the miracle drugs in those days that we have now, and it spread through the whole of my body. I was very ill indeed and I clearly remember the great pain I was in. I wasn't in bed but I was on pillows spread across two chairs downstairs in the little house we had. And I remember overhearing two doctors who examined me, and it was obvious from their whisperings they'd given up hope and thought I was going to die. They decided as a last resort to try giving me some form of carbolic acid. I looked that up in a medical dictionary only just recently, and it confirmed that in those days it really was used, but only very rarely, as a treatment. How they administered it to me, I don't remember. But they did, and then they went away.

And then after that I heard my mother whispering. She was praying, and she was offering God a bargain. She was saying if He'd save my life, she'd give him two more lives—have two more children, that is—in return. Well, He did save me, and so she kept her side of the bargain and she *did* have two more children! Isn't that just too funny? So I have a sister six years younger than me, and also a younger brother.

I can tell you I wasn't too pleased about it at the time, I thought I was going to be the baby of the family for good, and now here I was having to compete for attention. I was always quiet and I was a good little girl, and what little sins I had, well I was good at hiding those and letting my brother take the blame for things. He was the one who was a year and a half older than me, and he was supposed to be the one who had the brains in the family. He did, too. When he grew up he became a psychologist. I was always expected to keep up with him. It's something that my parents saw to, that the girls in the family went to school and had a good education. Many people aren't concerned about it for girls, for them the main thing is they should marry Jews when they grow up.

But my parents were different, and I did keep up with my brother. I did well in school, because it was expected of me, and I wanted to get praise. From school I went to the University of Wisconsin for three years and studied sociology, and from there transferred to the University of Chicago and spent a year there in the School of Social Service, which was one of the very few schools of social service there was in the country. I did a certain amount of graduate work, and then became a social worker. That was because it was then in the days of the Depression, and I had developed a social conscience, especially I should say more from my mother than from my father. It was her philosophy that you should never turn anyone in need away from your door, so I suppose I imbued some of that feeling, and from college too.

Wisconsin, you know, has always had the reputation of being a progressive state. They even had a senator named Bob LaFollette who ran for president in 1924 on a Progressive Party ticket. He was beaten by Calvin Coolidge, but he took nearly five million votes.

And maybe some of my mother's relatives who lived around where we did had an influence as well, though there's no one I specifically recall—not politically, I mean. But I do particularly remember knowing well one who was my uncle. He was my father's brother, and he was a gambler—that's how he made his living, by gambling. Of course we thought in our straitlaced family that was something to be ashamed of, so we never told people. But he was a really nice guy, who loved us as his children, not having any of his own. He was quite different from my father, who was a settled person.

Uncle Sam would often come and visit us, and he spent a lot of his time in a town on the border between Michigan and Wisconsin, where there were iron mines and lumber. The workers there liked to gamble their money weekends. He was great at bridge and poker and that kind of thing, and he usually used to win. I don't know the details of it, but he was often in the bucks, although sometimes he was absolutely broke, and had to come to our house and stay for a while until he recouped his fortunes. He would bring us presents of jewelry—not in a new jewelry box, he'd pick one out of his pocket and say "Here's something for you." We assumed they were gambling losses people had paid him that way for, or given him a ring off their finger. He brought me a beautiful emerald one time, and a gold ring, and he brought my kid sister wonderful jewelry, and my mother beautiful things too. We loved him very much, but we didn't talk about him to people who weren't within the family. Now isn't that silly?

I've always been particularly against war and worked in a lot of peace groups in my lifetime, and done things like marching against the war in Vietnam I don't know how many times during that period. I don't know what made me the way I am, but I seem always to have had the feeling that it's important for people to get together to fight against war and prejudice. Particularly racial prejudice, which might come from being Jewish and growing up in a small town where there was a lot of anti-Semitic feeling—though never any really overt acts, I have to say. I do remember one time when I was about nine at school, a boy chased me and called me a "sheeny," which is a derogatory anti-Semitic term. But I don't remember anything else except that I've always felt slightly different, a little bit in a way like an outsider. But also at school I had lots of friends I played with.

And of course as well I used to get into fights sometimes too with boys. But I was strong: there was a time when I was able to even lick the boys in my neighborhood. I have good muscle and I was stocky. It wasn't for calling me names we had fights though, I'm sure of that. But I didn't experience any real anti-Semitism, no, I can't say that I did. Well now: I was about seventeen when I graduated from high school, and in the fall I went to Wisconsin University as I said for three years, so I was about nineteen when I came to Chicago University social service school and twenty-one when I graduated from there. I knew all along that I wanted to be a social worker, because I believed you could help people that way, help them improve their lives. I worked for different authorities—the city, the county, the public-welfare department. Who was in charge kept changing all the time, and I changed with it. And it was while I was doing that that I met Louis.

Shall we take a break here? And you being an Englishman, would you like it if we had a cup of tea?

·   ·   ·

—The thing people most often ask me is how do I put up with him? Well you know, the answer to that is, he amuses me. In a million ways, he amuses me. I just appreciate his kind of humor, and he can tell the same story again and again, and I can hear it again and again—which of course after you've been married some fifty-five years or more you're bound to—and I like them all. I like the way he tells them. Nearly every time he changes them a little bit, you know—adds to them, takes away something. He does, he polishes them, and I enjoy hearing how he does it. In a way it's like going to a performance of an opera you're fond of and have seen over and over—you might know it inside out and back-wards, every word of it, but each time you see it and hear it you find something new in it.

Being married to Louis has been a great thing in my life, and I've never thought I'd want to be married to anyone else. I just consider myself very lucky that we found each other, I really do. So shall I tell you how we met? OK. We met through a theater group. We were both inter-ested in progressive politics if I might use that term, and at that time—this was in the thirties when I was a social worker—in the same office where I was, I had a woman friend named Janet. She was interested in taking acting classes, and she told me there was a theater group she and her husband went to, and she invited me to go with them. Shortly after that a young man came around our office doing some research work on welfare cases. I didn't notice him at the time and only discovered later his name had been Louis Terkel. He doesn't remember it apparently either.

Well, I went to the theater class with my friend and her husband, and we did a scene from a play called *Ethan Frome,* which is adapted from a novel by Edith Wharton. We were doing the reading of it and talking about it in the theater lobby, and this rather short dark fella passed by.

He had black hair then—oh dear—and it was Louis. He was wearing a hat pulled down over his eyes and his coat collar was turned up. It was February and not very warm so maybe he was about to leave. I thought he looked like a hoodlum, and I wondered how he'd got into the place and what he was doing there. But he'd overheard us reading and talking about the play, and he came over and said he'd just been in New York and he'd seen it performed professionally, and he thought it was wonderful. So I thought well the guy might look like a hood but he didn't talk like one.

My connection with the theater meant I saw Studs from time to time, and of course we found we had a lot in common—including, I must say, our age. I'm exactly one week older than he is! We had what you might call the same historical frame of reference too about things, things that were happening in our time, and our outlook on them was the same. Away from politics also we were the same. I remember he took me to a movie at an art house—that was actually our first date. It was a French film with a wonderful actress in it whose name I've forgotten—but I *do* remember I was very impressed by his good taste! It was called *Club des Femmes*. And then we went out on some more dates and at the time—I think both before and after we were married—there were quite a few good Russian films around—*The Battleship Potemkin, Ten Days That Shook the World* and a number of other less famous ones.

We saw quite a few of them, and we had our own personal little joke from them. In Russian films the hero and heroine didn't embrace, they shook hands on meeting or parting. So we used to do the same, like this—"Natasha! Aloushka!" "Ah—Natasha! Ah—Aloushka!" with a very hearty handshake to show affection.

There was much sympathy towards the Soviet Union in general in those times, a feeling that good things could happen and might happen. Nothing was known about the bad things that were going on then. Lincoln Steffens, the much-admired and highly respected American journalist, had visited Lenin's Russia and written afterwards his famous phrase about it, "I have seen the future and it works," and that pretty well summed up the atmosphere.

I think both Louis and I decided together we'd get married, but Louis always says it was because he owed me money. In my job as a social worker I was well paid, and he certainly wasn't making what I was, and he always kept borrowing from me when we went anywhere. In those days the man always paid, so he was borrowing twenty dollars or thirty dollars each time, and when we married he owed me twenty dollars, so he says that's why he married me, to cancel the debt.

In fact he's never known how to handle money. I don't mean by that that he's profligate or spendthrift, which he isn't—it's just that the subject never interests him. So it's always been that I handle our affairs to do with finance, I do our tax returns and so on. We have just the one checkbook, and I give him whatever cash he needs when he needs it. I don't do it very well because I'm not good at all with figures. But somebody has to try and keep some sense of order or it would be impossible.

There was a time once when briefly, for financial reasons, I had to go back to work. This was when Louis was blacklisted, and our fortunes had sunk very low indeed. I decided I'd maybe get to be a schoolteacher, so I went to a training college for a semester, but then instead I worked in a child-care center, which I loved. The director of it asked me to go there as a part-time social worker, and it was a good place, an agency of the Episcopalian Diocese of Chicago. But then things started to improve for us, so I quit.

That time, though, when the blacklisting happened to us, was a very traumatizing experience. We first heard of it when we had a phone call at three o'clock in the morning from a friend, who had just heard that someone in Hollywood—a writer—had named Studs Terkel. I remember shaking and trembling because I knew it was going to affect our lives profoundly, and it did. I can still remember that feeling of fear. Louis had a number of jobs on radio, and a television show, *Studs' Place,* which had completed a successful series and we were very hopeful it was going to come back again. We weren't living in luxury, we had rather a modest apartment and we had a little savings, but we knew from then on things would be very difficult. The only people who would give him a job were WFMT Radio who put him on once a week. And after all this time he's still with them of course. But then, in those days, that was the only regular income we had, and we only just about avoided having to borrow from the family and relatives.

The hysteria didn't catch on in Chicago the way it did on the two coasts, especially California, and it didn't affect our relationship with our close friends: they were very supportive. But there were a few people who were nasty, such as a man who was with the American Legion. He was on what they called their Loyalty Committee, and if he heard Louis had got a job somewhere or other to go out and put on an evening entertainment for some organization, he would call them up and say "Don't have him!" Louis would try to make a joke of it, and he wrote to him one time and said "After they heard from you, they doubled my fee for the occasion." But it did hurt him. There was always the fear that the hysteria might grow, and of not knowing what might happen next when you were stigmatized like that. But luckily McCarthy overreached himself, and fell out of favor.

Other than then, when I had to, no I've never felt I wanted to go back to work, life has always been so busy and full, especially for me when our son was small. I've never had a hobby, though I'd love to have been a writer myself. I read a lot—a lot of political stuff of course, because I like to know what's going on—and Studs' books, well I haven't only read all of them but I've *heard* all of them. He reads them to me—every interview, every word—as he finishes each one. I get to hear it right away. So I hear the whole of every book as it comes along. And he's a good reader, so I enjoy it.

There are so many of his interviews, that I couldn't pick out one as my very favorite. But I could choose one of his radio interviews, there's one of those that even though it was oh ten years ago at least now, I still remember it as my most favorite one of all. It was with Maestro Joseph Krips, the orchestral conductor, who's sadly since died. Krips was telling him about a time after the war when he got an orchestra together—I think it was in Vienna—and life was very grim, and some talented musicians came together just to play some Mozart. They all loved Mozart: I do too, he's my most favorite composer. And Krips was talking about him to Studs and he said "You know, Beethoven—he sometimes reached Heaven. But Mozart—he came from Heaven!" And I was so touched by that, I was so moved! I've never ever forgotten it.

Well, to go back to his book interviews, I've had the rare experience, I think you could say privilege, of having sat in just a few times on some of those. As you know, Louis doesn't drive, and he wanted to go and talk to some farmers somebody'd told him about, who lived in Iowa and North Dakota and South Dakota, and hear what they were going through because they were having a hard time. He asked me if I'd drive him around up there, and I said I would but only on condition he did the map reading and piloted us. He said he'd never done anything like that in his life, so I told him he'd have to learn how, which he eventually did.

We made a few wrong moves, but we eventually got to see who we were looking for.

There was one interview he did, God, even now it almost makes me cry thinking about it. I can't remember the farmer's name, but he and his wife were sitting in their living room, and there was a big grandfather clock ticking away. And the old farmer was sitting there remembering, and there was a neighboring farmer there too, and they were commiserating with each other about what they were going to do, because they were losing their farms, they weren't making a living. And the neighbor said "What we need is a good war to get us out of this." And the other one said "We had a good war—and I lost my son. I lost my son in the Second World War." And he started to cry—and his wife cried—and I cried—and we all sat there crying. Oh dear. That's what war's all about, isn't it? Excuse me.

Oh yes, I have noticed certain things about the way he interviews, things that get people talking to him, that he's probably not aware of. One is that he often takes on the actual rhythm, the speech cadence, of the person he's talking with. Or sometimes he might unconsciously imitate a slight accent the other person doesn't realize they have. It's the feeling of empathy he has with them that enables him to do it, and I think it makes the other person feel closer and that he's easier to talk to. If it's someone from the South, Louis gets a slight Southern accent himself without realizing it. I don't remember noticing it at the time, but it wouldn't surprise me now if I heard it again to notice that he'd taken on a slight German accent in the interviews with Krips I was telling you about. Isn't that interesting?

And I do think that word sums everything up for me really—"interesting." I feel very happy that I met Louis and married him, because life has certainly not been dull. We've had a very nondull marriage indeed. Is that a term, "nondull"? Anyway, we've had an interesting marriage, and part of it I suppose is that I can say I've tried to stay out of his way in the sense that when he's wanted to do something I've gone along with it. Sometimes I scold Louis about things he does or doesn't do, and there've been failures in my life, and things that make me sad. I'd like to go on talking about them but off the record, please.

Roger Smith

We met, we talked, and we discussed everything except what we would discuss if he agreed to do a tape-recorded interview. That, I said, I would leave entirely to him—and if I asked him any question during it which he didn't want to answer, he should merely say "I don't want to talk about that" and the subject wouldn't be pursued. He has changed his name—but not to the one I have given him here.

He lived on his own in a small and comfortably furnished apartment in the northwest of the city. A tall, well-built man with receding hair, he had a kindly, thoughtful voice and an easy manner. He wore slacks and an open-necked check shirt. His sitting room was compact, with subdued lighting: a television set on a low table in a corner, and near it a record player with a large collection of LPs and CDs. All the walls were lined with shelves of books. Among them were three paperbacks standing together: Young Lonigan, The Young Manhood of Studs Lonigan, *and* Judgment Day *by James T. Farrell. Next to them was a copy of* Hard Times.

—Yes I'm entirely happy with the name you've chosen to give me, because it really does truly protect my anonymity. I've changed my name from Terkel as you know, and the fact that what I've changed it to isn't "Roger Smith" is very good, because that doesn't reveal my alias either. Calling me by the name of the hotel you're to be staying in New York— well, that's quite witty I think, if you don't mind me saying so.

So where will I begin? Would you like some more of that cranberry juice? Yes it is rather good isn't it? OK, well now let's see. I'm forty-nine years of age going on fifty, and I work for a big accountancy firm here in Chicago. I've always been a very detail-oriented person, and I enjoy the work, but it doesn't really enable me to be as creative as I'd like to be. But from a purely pragmatic standpoint, I find it a manner in which I can make a decent living.

I'd have liked to have been a writer. I enjoy writing—particularly humorous writing and social satire. But I've always tended to be a prag- matist and being practical about it I've never been under the illusion that I'd be able to make a living at it. So I've kept it as a sideline, and I decided years ago that accountancy would be the most practical course to follow to make a decent living.

I think when I was a young boy I did envision myself as a writer—but even then I figured having one writer in the family would probably make the odds against my becoming a success even heavier. And then again of course when I was a kid, my father was struggling, so it was a difficult situation, when I come to think about it. In fact for all the time I was living at home, which was until I was twenty or twenty-one—well, it wasn't until after I left home, and I was off on my own as an adult, that things really began to click for my father.

Of course he encountered wide problems because of his political beliefs, and I do admire him that he was very principled about them. I share many of those beliefs myself. In that respect he never compromised, and it probably kept him from being financially successful for many years. But it did mean that he was able to live with himself. Not having too much money never really bothered me. I mean there were a lot of things I was unhappy about as a kid, but that wasn't one of them. I never regretted not being from a well-to-do family, which we weren't at that time, and I never felt I had to put on any airs about it.

I've never been married. I've come close on a number of occasions, and had any number of women friends over the years. I still have a number I've known for twenty-five or thirty years, and I've kept in contact with a couple of very close women friends who themselves have never been married, and we still sustain that friendship. But I guess a fair assessment would be to say I'm an independent-minded person who's always been hesitant to get tied down emotionally, and I haven't really wanted to make a commitment to marriage or to having a family.

I think it wouldn't be totally out of the question eventually, but at my age . . . well I wouldn't say I'm set in my ways, it *could* happen. But as far as starting a family goes, that's something I would have to give serious consideration about. But of course I could meet a divorced woman with kids, that's always possible. I'm sure there are men who become fathers at age fifty and beyond, but I'm not sure it would be a comfortable role for me.

It's fair to say I think that as far as my personal life is concerned I've always been independent and made my own decisions. Very independent—possibly even a little headstrong sometimes. Though not at all in my job, where I do have managerial responsibility—but where top-down decision making is the very antithesis of what I believe in.

Something I've always regretted is I never took music lessons at school when I was a kid, and so I can't read music. I'd like to have learned to play the violin. There was a school orchestra, and I did have aspirations at high school of joining it. But when I tried to, it was in my second year, and I was told it was too late, I should have begun in my freshman year, so my ambitions were scotched. It was a public high school where I was one of twenty-eight hundred students, and we'd been left pretty much to our own devices when we started, under rather mediocre and uncaring teachers. Very few of them showed much interest in the students.

But although I can't play, or read, music, I do enjoy listening to it, especially when I'm working at a solitary task. My tastes are on the whole classical, particularly of the traditional kind—Beethoven, Brahms, Mozart. And I'd throw in Dvořák as well, because there's a certain bittersweet quality about his work that I find attractive. Of course I like his *From the New World* Symphony, but also I'm very fond of his Eighth Symphony too, it's very lyrical and it's not heard as often as the others. I'm not into opera so much, with a few exceptions like *Traviata*, which I like despite the fact that it's all about privileged folks who have no goal in life except party party partying all the time. Wagner I can't endure.

And my other great pleasure is, as I say, in reading. It includes a lot of fairly contemporary authors. Nelson Algren is one, have you heard of him? He's one of my very favorite writers, I like the way he endows his characters with a great deal of humanity in a way few other authors can. He brings out all their foibles and characteristics, and their strengths as well. From what I understand he has more of a reputation in Europe than he has here—here it's not always necessarily a positive one either. Someone else I like is Isaac Bashevis Singer. He wrote wonderfully well about the immigrant experience in his novels and short stories, but he took a tremendous interest in the supernatural as well. His characters included demons and dybbuks. Of course I like classical authors too, I've never really immersed myself in him but I've read a fair amount of Shakespeare. And I've enjoyed Dostoyevsky—if you can use that world "enjoy" about Dostoyevsky.

I've also done a fair amount of volunteer work, but I'd rather not elaborate. It would reveal my identity.

Yes, I do read my father's books, I think I've read most of them. The one I think I probably enjoyed most was the one which I believe was one of the least successful, *Talking to Myself.* It didn't follow his usual format, it was sort of a random, personal memoir for the most part, kind of free-form association. I guess I would say that would be one of my favorites. And an earlier oral history he did, *Division Street: America,* that would be another of my favorites too. He titled it in a metaphorical sense, but even today there are a lot of folks who believe he was writing about the street in Chicago actually called "Division Street."

To revert to this same matter for a moment, about the earlier book we were talking about, *Talking to Myself.* It's often referred to as my father's autobiography, which of course it isn't—or at least only to a degree. It's much more of a meander of reminiscences about people he's met, and chiefly only about himself as the bystander or spectator. I guess I've picked up some of that attitude to life myself to a great extent. I have a tendency to store memories of absurd incidents and of offbeat characters in my mind the same way he does.

When I hear people talking about his work, which happens occasionally, I don't divulge my identity. But it's a weird experience. I'm not recalling any specific incident, but when it's happened I've never wanted the people concerned to know who I was. I mean I'm not resentful of my father, but in our society the cult of celebrity is so pervasive that as often as not I get the feeling that those of us who are related to celebrities tend to be diminished in the process. I can recall incidents even when I was a kid at high school, when people who knew of the relationship would say "This is so-and-so," and then of me "And this is so-and-so the son of." And I would say "Why is that necessary? It's quite unnecessary to say that. You don't introduce your other friends and say who their fathers are. It's not customary to do that, so why do you insist on introducing me that way?" I really resented it.

All along, I would have preferred my identity not to be known at school, but unfortunately the name was not a very common one. My mother was in the parent-teacher association so of course was constantly being asked if Studs Terkel was her husband—and the parents told their children, and so there was no way I had of escaping it. The only way I can put it is to say that throughout my entire school life I felt captive, and the victim of over-high expectations from the teachers. It wasn't done deliberately or out of malice, but it was due to insensitivity. When I did well at something, I was given little credit because it was almost expected that I would, and was taken for granted. When I didn't do so well, well I hadn't lived up to expectations. It was a no-win situation.

The result was that it discouraged me from really trying at anything—and still did, later, from trying to cultivate my writing skills. I still do write, as I said, as relaxation and to a degree for entertainment. And I use the ability I have at work, too—I've written training material for businesses, and they read well though I say it myself, and they've been well received by those who've read them. But if I did try and take a different direction—well, I feel comparison would always be inevitable, and there'd be no way I could escape it.

That's one of the principal reasons—no, it's *the* principal reason—that I go to great lengths to conceal my identity, because it still applies. I want absolutely to be my own person. Of course not by any means all the people I work with know who my father is anyway, I mean they've never heard of him: but of those who have, not one of them is aware of his relationship to me.

I think it would most definitely have helped if I'd had at least one brother or sister, and that's a situation that I've always regretted, that I haven't. There's no doubt at all in my mind that the pressure would have been less.

I can't think of anything I've said to you this evening that I would want to take out of our conversation. But the truth is that I don't feel after a long working day I've been quite at my best, and if the circumstances had been different it might have been better. But if I could see the transcript before you use it, there may be things I'd like to elaborate on, if I may, and perhaps just put in some extra thoughts that would make it mutually satisfying? Thank you, it's been a pleasure meeting you.

Appendices

A Letter from up North, from C. J. Pomeroy

Some I-Don't-Mind-If-You-Use-It-But-I'd-Prefer-You-Not-
to-Say-It-Was-Me-Who-Told-You-Its
(None of Them Are Members
of His Family Though)

A Letter from up North,
from C. J. Pomeroy

Dear Tony,

Sorry to hear of all your troubles. But don't worry, something'll turn up—like your Oscar Wilde said, even if it's only the noses of your friends.

Well, I've been doing what you asked me to, and in the last year I've been hunting through all the newspaper and journal book-review files I could find, reading what negative criticisms have been made over the years of the work of your friend Mr S Terkel. You're only too right that not many folk have had much to say that wasn't in his favor. Seems like every time he publishes a new book, there's a chorus of hallelujahs most everyone of note runs to be first to get in there with. No surprise, say I—I like his things a lot myself too.

All I've been able to find is the occasional sourpuss remark here and there some place, as a rule from some cobwebby academic whose main gripe seems to be folk actually find Terkel *readable*—so therefore you can't help feeling their own stuff isn't, and hasn't attracted the same amount of attention they feel it's due. You also get the odd gibe like there's nothing too clever about switching on a tape recorder and putting down on paper the words people say on tape. I can't believe anybody really thinks that's all that *does* happen, and willfully chooses to ignore the much-more-work transcribing, editing, arranging, and the rest.

However, without naming names, as you suggest, I've gathered the criticisms of his work into some roughly similar categories.

Firstly, some say—though at most not more than two or three—that anything of his is a 'non-book'. Those who write it never actually define what a 'non-book' is, so I'm not too sure what they mean. I *think* what they mean includes the 'just switching on a tape recorder' bullshit mentioned above, plus the fact it doesn't have shape or form and merely goes on for a while and then stops. I guess their idea of a 'proper' book is one that has literary tone throughout ('Essays of Elia' perhaps?) I don't know. Whatever, it shouldn't be like Mr Terkel's.

Another thing some people—again, 'some' meaning like three or three and a half perhaps—object to, is he takes his questions out. Why this should cause grief I don't know. I think somebody told me—you, was it?—that he does it not to stand between speaker and reader. But the general beef seems to be he might be asking some pretty loaded questions so as to get pretty loaded answers. (Example: Question—Were things bad during the Depression? Answer—Yeah, things were bad during the Depression. There you are, see, he took out his question and got them to say things were bad during the Depression.)

It's usually the right-wingers who charge him with question-dropping. And they usually say it's to produce answers to backup his own left-wing leanings. Some go further and say not only he does that, but before he even starts interviewing, he picks out people to talk to he knows are going to give him the 'lefty' material he wants. I don't see how anyone who has read *The Good War* could accuse him of that, because it includes interviews with people whose views are diametrically opposed to each other's, and there's no way *he* could hold them all at once himself.

Somebody else wrote he was forever putting forward a sentimental picture of the innate goodness of the common man; someone else said he chose people only for their entertainment value (I detected a note of the criticism of him as being 'readable' here); and someone very lofty wrote he found Terkel 'boring'. Oh dear, what a vivid life he himself must lead!

One academic wrote sternly that Terkel ought to 'analyze' his material. What in hell can he have meant by that? Mini-tables showing that of those interviewed, 42% had pleasant dreams, 37% had nightmares, 21% never remembered dreaming or, if they did, weren't going to confess what it was they dreamed about?

About the one and only criticism of his work I came across that made me stop and think (but only for about half a minute) was one that said he didn't think Terkel gave people long enough time to think about what they were going to say, and that therefore what they were reported as saying wasn't necessarily 'valid'. But when I thought about this myself, I thought (a) well, how does he know Terkel doesn't give them long enough? Surely they know he's coming, or does the guy imagine Terkel just rushes up to people in the street and starts asking them questions? And (b) how long is 'long enough'? An hour? A day? A week? And (c) if I have a long time myself to think what I'm going to say to someone, it mightn't necessarily be more 'valid' (whatever that means), because I might decide on reflection not to say something I really felt.

So there you are Tony, that's about the best I can do for you, and I realise it's not very much. But as I wrote you at the beginning of this letter, your friend Mr T really does have praise in cascades each new book he does—and in my opinion he sure deserves it.

By the way, how's your friend Mary Loudon who you introduced me and Bishop Eric to when we were last in London? The Bishop said he really fancied her—but of course don't tell her that!

Best,

Cyril.

Some I-Don't-Mind-If-You-Use-It-But-I'd-Prefer-You-Not-to-Say-It-Was-Me-Who-Told-You-Its (None of Them Are Members of His Family Though)

1.—The first thing he has to do when he gets into work mornings is go to the bathroom. He comes in through the swing doors, then walks across the lobby past the reception desk. He doesn't say anything to anybody, just goes on down the corridor the other side and disappears. After around ten minutes or so, he reappears, then it's "Hi! How're you doin'?" to the receptionist and anyone else he meets, and he ambles away off to his office down the other corridor.

Three or four times a day he visits the bathroom again. Everybody he

passes in the corridors, whether he knows them or not, whether he's ever
even seen them in his life before, he says "Hi! I'm going to the john."
It's like a flight announcement, "The *Studs Terkel* now departing along
the east side corridor is off to the john," you know?

Once in there, he goes in one of the cubicles. They have doors and
walls down to only about a foot up from the ground, and reach a little
over head high when you're standing up. If he's gone in the bathroom
with someone else he continues their conversation from in there. No
matter if there are two or three other occupied cubicles, he goes on
talking about whatever it was. If you go in and he's on his own, you'll
hear him talking to himself. You see this pair of feet and the trousers
round their ankles, and he's saying "Are you trying to tell me *Othello* isn't
a greater opera than *Aïda*?" I joined in on a conversation he was having
like that with himself one time, but he never noticed, he just continued
it, including me in it. After I'd rinsed my fingers and dried them I walked
out, and I guess he never noticed, just went on talking with himself
again.

2.—Nobody will ever know just how much Ida underpins his life, apart
from her—and himself, if he ever tells her about it. Without her, he'd be
totally lost. When she had to go in hospital to have that big heart operation a few years back, it almost destroyed him, he couldn't function or
carry on his daily life at all. He'd go to his office in the morning, look
through his mail, then without speaking a word to anyone he'd go out
again. He'd take the elevator down to the lobby, go to the cabstand
outside, and be driven straight to the hospital. He'd go to Ida's bedside,
and just sit there looking at her, holding her hand. He wouldn't move,
he wouldn't eat, and the only sustenance he had was he'd take a slug
now and again from a bottle of Scotch he had in his pocket. He'd stay
there like that for as long as they'd let him in the evening, until he was
absolutely zonked. Then they'd lift him into a wheelchair and take him
down and put him in a cab and send him home. This went on a week or
more I guess. One time during it I called him up around midnight—I
knew he wouldn't be sleeping—to ask him how things were and how Ida
was coming along. I guess he thought it was the hospital, because he
grabbed the phone to answer it pretty well at the first ring. I started
asking him a few things, but all he said was yes or no a couple of times.

Then I heard a strange sort of sound coming over the phone, and he very suddenly hung up on me. And you know what? I realized he was crying.

3.—When he's in New York, he plays a game with everybody—and it took years before I found out it *was* a game. He'll call you up and he'll say "Hi, why don't you and your wife come have dinner with Ida and me at the Algonquin Tuesday night?" Or if he's short on time it'll be "Say, why don't you come for coffee Saturday morning at the Algonquin?" And when you go there all the staff and waiters and everybody are all falling about to look after him, it's "Yes certainly Mr. Terkel," "Your table's ready now Mr. Terkel, if you'd like to come through," and in the lobby as he passes the desk the clerk calls out "Oh Mr. Terkel there's a message for you sir" and all the rest of it. So naturally you assume that's where he's staying and is so well known there because that's where he always stays. It comes as quite a shock to you if you eventually find out, as I did, that not only he's not staying there, what's more he's never stayed there in his life. Naturally the Algonquin don't mind people thinking they're his home-from-home in New York, but why he should want to give that impression, or where he and Ida really *do* stay, I've no idea at all. It can't be snobbishness, because Studs just isn't that kind of a person, no way, ever. It's part of his determination always to keep a part of himself private, I guess.

4.—In the Terkels' home, in a very nice residential neighborhood in the north of the city, in the downstairs bathroom (or washroom, or rest room, or toilet—my goodness, what a variety of euphemisms these Americans have for their lavatories!) on one of the walls there's a framed cartoon—from the *New Yorker* it looks like—and it's a picture of a scowling heavily built man sitting in an armchair in his shirtsleeves, saying to his wife who's crossing the room to answer what's the obviously ringing telephone "If that's Studs Terkel, there's a good few things I want to get off my chest!"

5.—He used to be a neighbor of mine, and I often used to see him walking along the street deeply engaged in conversation with himself. He would talk with himself, and argue with himself: and every now and again he'd stop, look up at the sky, throw up his hands and talk in a louder voice. Then his hands and his voice would come down, and he'd go on walking and talking "normally" again. I happened to ask him one day at a party at a friend's house if he knew he did it, and why he did it. He grinned and he said, "Oh sure I talk to myself, and it's because I'm such a good listener." One funny thing about it as well was that not far away from us there was a home for people who were—well, you know, funny in the head—and sometimes you'd see one of them walking along the street behaving exactly the same way. And when you saw Studs doing it, it gave you a kind of weird feeling sometimes, and you'd think "Well I wonder if those people are all that strange after all?" Wasn't there a psychiatrist in the sixties called R. D. Laing who wrote a book called *The Divided Self* about this sort of thing?

6.—Studs doesn't exactly steal other people's stories and pretend they involved him, but he's not averse to retelling them as though he'd been present when they happened. I remember some years ago now, I was at a party given by Leonard Bernstein in his New York apartment, and I was talking in a corner with Lillian Hellman the playwright. She wasn't drunk but she'd had a few drinks, and she was waving her arms about rather a lot while she talked. The place was crowded with people all chattering and laughing like they do on these occasions, and Studs was there—but he was way way over the other side of the big crowded room. In fact from where we were, you could hardly see him. Leonard Bernstein pushed his way through the throng over to us, to see how we were doing, and just as he got behind Lillian, who was smoking a cigarette, she flung back her arm and it caught him on the cheek. He couldn't help it, he winced and drew back, and she turned round, and seeing what she'd done was horrified and she said "Oh Lennie, Lennie, I'm so sorry." You know, something like that. And without hesitation, Bernstein took her hand in his, and he said "Lillian, being burned by you is like being kissed by a beautiful woman!" Well the next day I repeated this story to Studs—and then about two years later, I heard him tell it, exactly the same, word for word, as though he'd been there when it happened. In spite of his fabulous memory, he'd forgotten to say he was telling it in front of the person he'd got it from. He can't let a good story, or a chance of telling it, go by. But that's no great sin, I guess.

7.—Oh it's really so sad the way his hearing's deteriorating the way it is now. Inevitable, I suppose. He tries to make a joke of it, swears and curses about his hearing aids, one in each ear, says they're not working properly, bawls out "I'm bionic man!", is all the time fiddling around with them until they start giving out whistling noises, and then yells "What the hell's the matter with these goddam things?" and smacks them around. And this is the man who's spent his lifetime listening out for the nuances in people's speech, exactly whether they used an "um" or an "ah" or an "er," and the differences in meaning between them. It's so ironic isn't it?

8.—He and I, we've known each other more than forty years, and I can tell you in all honesty, in all that time he's never ever even tried to make a pass at me. And I can tell you that when he was younger, and also when he was older than younger, he was always very attractive to women—and I mean very. He was good-looking, but much more important than that, he had that thing, you know, the kind of energy and fizz about him, I suppose what's called dynamism that's very attractive to women, the sort of power thing inside of him. Above all he had the one quality that I think most women find irresistible, which was he made you laugh. Combine all that in one package like he did, and wow! I hope you don't think I'm saying that in any way I regret he never made a pass at me, because I'm not. All I am saying is that I guess if he ever had, well I would have resisted it a while. Like thirty seconds or so.

Acknowledgments

As well as the many people who were willing and enthusiastic to talk to me about Studs Terkel, and did—often lavishing food and drink on me as well—many others gave me much help in arranging meetings, providing information and contacts, and assisting me in a variety of ways.

Photographer Jennifer Girard and her aide, Nicole, went to great trouble on my behalf, and so did Roger Lewin. I owe special thanks to Linda Lewis for all the extra work she did for me; and Judy Marriott at the *Chicago Tribune* did me a great favor. I thank too Brooke Palmer in Boston. Joan and Bob Morrison of Morristown, New Jersey, gave my wife and me wonderful hospitality in their home, and tracked down and sent to me a special book I wanted.

At my American publishers, Henry Holt and Company, Inc., Bill Strachan was a kind and understanding editor; and at HarperCollins in England, Richard Johnson has been as meticulous and supportive as ever.

In England, where most of the tape-transcribing and writing of the book was done, Janet Bayliss at the Suffolk County Library went to endless trouble to research background material for me most promptly and efficiently. And, as ever, Linda Ginn typed and retyped and arranged and rearranged the manuscript with speed and unfailing good humor.

My wife Margery transcribed most of the tapes, taking on this burden with calmness and pleasure, and at the same time still gave me as she always does her love and care.

Tony Parker
Westleton, Suffolk, England